HAL•LEONARD®
GUITAR PLAY-ALONG

AUDIO ACCESS INCLUDED

MORE **STEVIE RAY VAUGHAN**

VOL. 140

PLAYBACK+
Speed • Pitch • Balance • Loop

To access audio visit:
www.halleonard.com/mylibrary

Enter Code
3616-6842-8693-1218

Cover photo © Andrea Laubach / Retna

ISBN 978-1-4584-0549-4

HAL•LEONARD®
CORPORATION
7777 W. BLUEMOUND RD. P.O. BOX 13819 MILWAUKEE, WI 53213

Visit Hal Leonard Online at
www.halleonard.com

GUITAR NOTATION LEGEND

THE MUSICAL STAFF shows pitches and rhythms and is divided by bar lines into measures. Pitches are named after the first seven letters of the alphabet.

TABLATURE graphically represents the guitar fingerboard. Each horizontal line represents a string, and each number represents a fret.

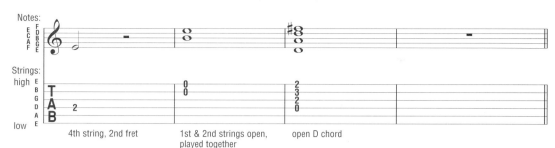

4th string, 2nd fret   1st & 2nd strings open, played together   open D chord

HALF-STEP BEND: Strike the note and bend up 1/2 step.

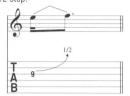

WHOLE-STEP BEND: Strike the note and bend up one step.

GRACE NOTE BEND: Strike the note and immediately bend up as indicated.

SLIGHT (MICROTONE) BEND: Strike the note and bend up 1/4 step.

BEND AND RELEASE: Strike the note and bend up as indicated, then release back to the original note. Only the first note is struck.

PRE-BEND: Bend the note as indicated, then strike it.

VIBRATO: The string is vibrated by rapidly bending and releasing the note with the fretting hand.

PALM MUTING: The note is partially muted by the pick hand lightly touching the string(s) just before the bridge.

HAMMER-ON: Strike the first (lower) note with one finger, then sound the higher note (on the same string) with another finger by fretting it without picking.

PULL-OFF: Place both fingers on the notes to be sounded. Strike the first note and without picking, pull the finger off to sound the second (lower) note.

LEGATO SLIDE: Strike the first note and then slide the same fret-hand finger up or down to the second note. The second note is not struck.

SHIFT SLIDE: Same as legato slide, except the second note is struck.

TRILL: Very rapidly alternate between the notes indicated by continuously hammering on and pulling off.

TAPPING: Hammer ("tap") the fret indicated with the pick-hand index or middle finger and pull off to the note fretted by the fret hand.

NATURAL HARMONIC: Strike the note while the fret-hand lightly touches the string directly over the fret indicated.

PINCH HARMONIC: The note is fretted normally and a harmonic is produced by adding the edge of the thumb or the tip of the index finger of the pick hand to the normal pick attack.

TREMOLO PICKING: The note is picked as rapidly and continuously as possible.

VIBRATO BAR DIVE AND RETURN: The pitch of the note or chord is dropped a specified number of steps (in rhythm), then returned to the original pitch.

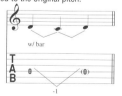

VIBRATO BAR SCOOP: Depress the bar just before striking the note, then quickly release the bar.

VIBRATO BAR DIP: Strike the note and then immediately drop a specified number of steps, then release back to the original pitch.

Additional Musical Definitions

 (accent)
- Accentuate note (play it louder).

 (staccato)
- Play the note short.

D.S. al Coda
- Go back to the sign (𝄋), then play until the measure marked "*To Coda*," then skip to the section labelled "*Coda*."

D.C. al Fine
- Go back to the beginning of the song and play until the measure marked "*Fine*" (end).

Fill

N.C.

- Label used to identify a brief melodic figure which is to be inserted into the arrangement.

- Harmony is implied.

- Repeat measures between signs.

- When a repeated section has different endings, play the first ending only the first time and the second ending only the second time.

HAL•LEONARD

GUITAR PLAY-ALONG

MORE
STEVIE RAY VAUGHAN

VOL. 140

CONTENTS

Ain't Gone 'n' Give Up on Love

Written by Stevie Ray Vaughan

Tune down 1/2 step:
(low to high) E♭-A♭-D♭-G♭-B♭-E♭

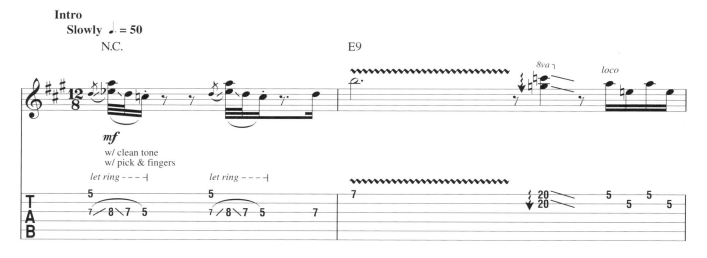

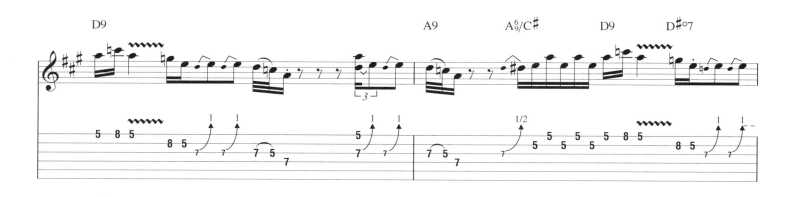

Love _____ won't give up on __ me.

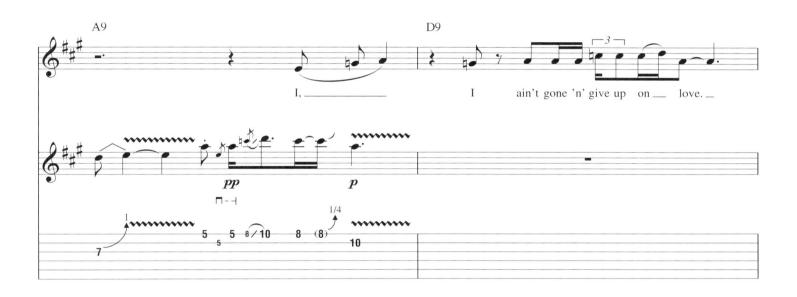

I, _____ I ain't gone 'n' give up on __ love. __

Love _____ ain't gon' give up on __ me. _____

5

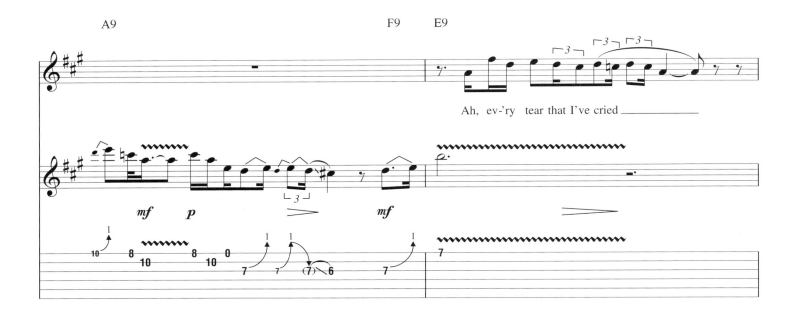

Ah, ev-'ry tear that I've cried _____

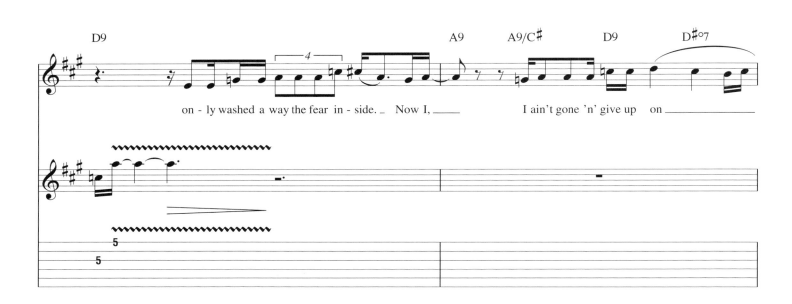

on - ly washed a way the fear in - side. _ Now I, _____ I ain't gone 'n' give up on _____

Verse

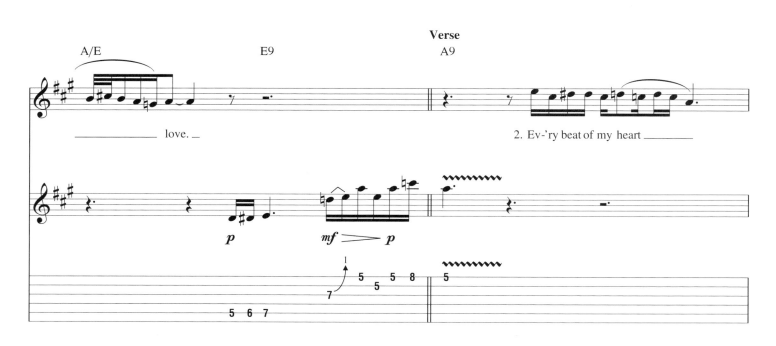

_____ love. _ 2. Ev'ry beat of my heart _____

pounds _ with joy ___ 'n' not with pain. _____

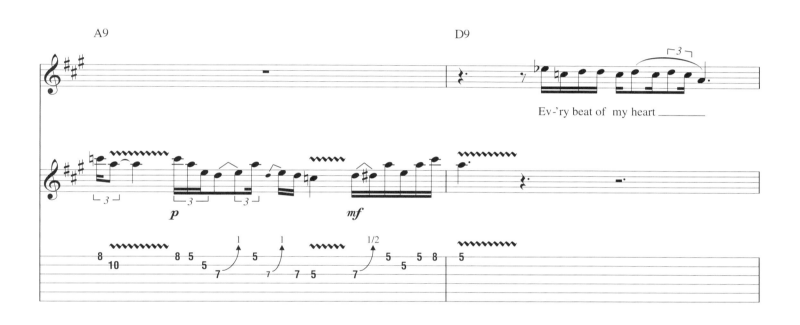

Ev-'ry beat of my heart _____

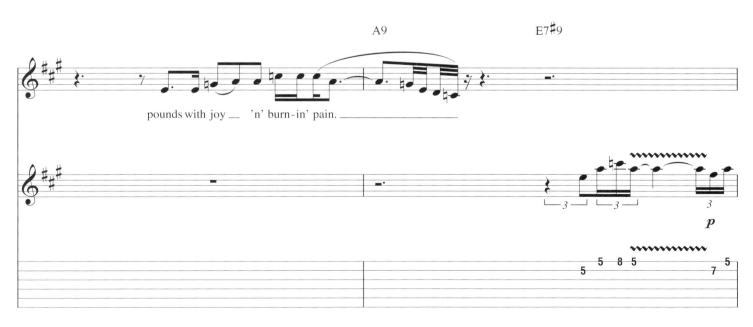

pounds with joy __ 'n' burn-in' pain. _____

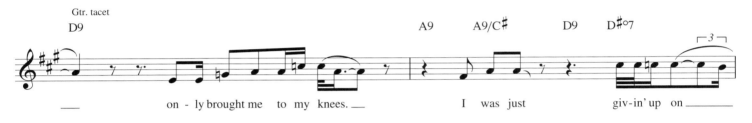

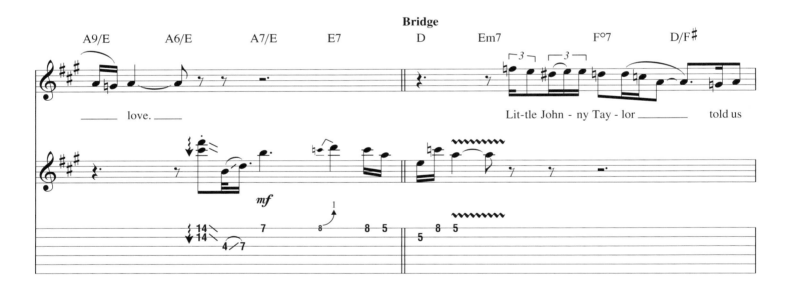

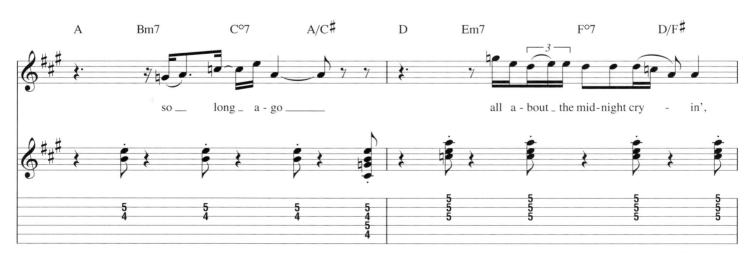

whoa, _ 'n' that you been ly-in'.   What a - bout the price __   that   will, _

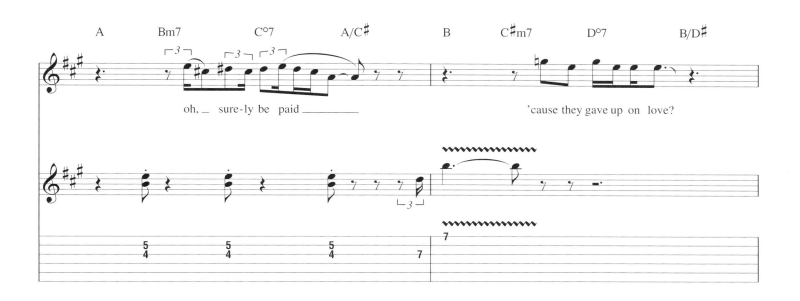

oh, __ sure-ly be paid _____   'cause they gave up on love?

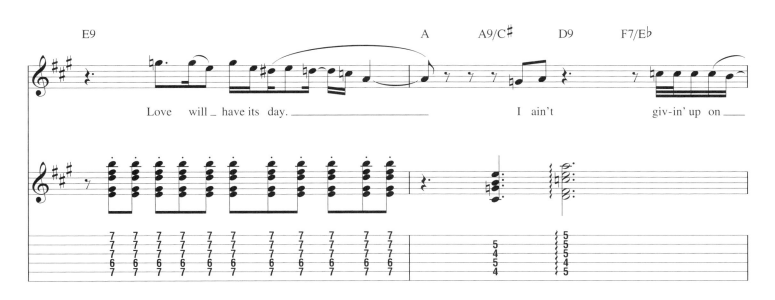

Love   will _ have its day. _____   I ain't   giv-in' up on ___

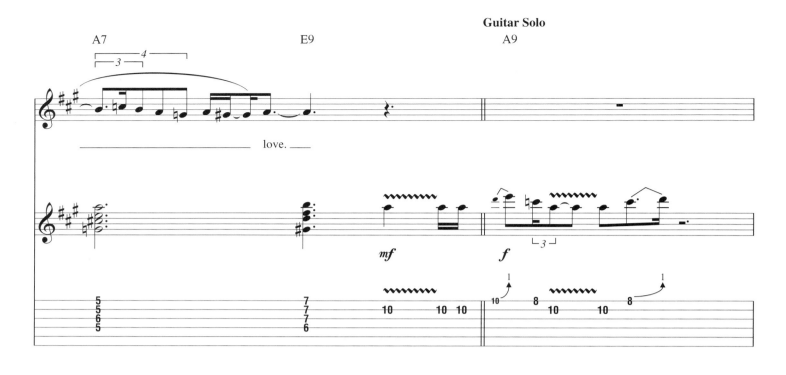

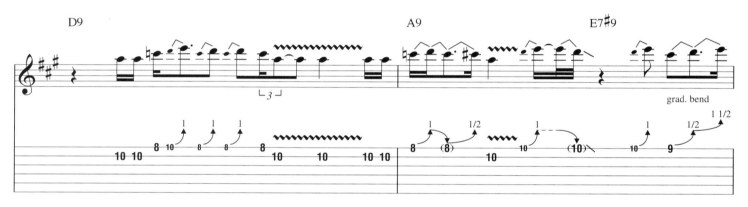

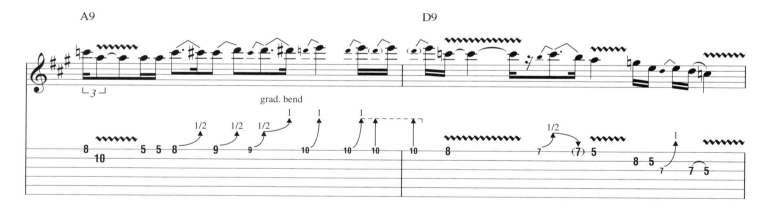

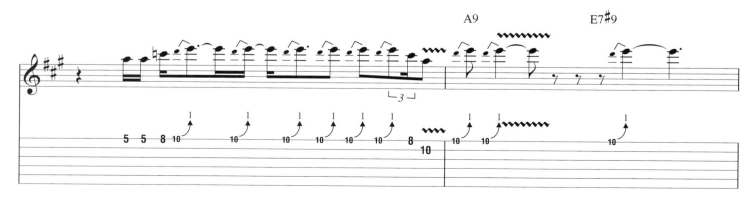

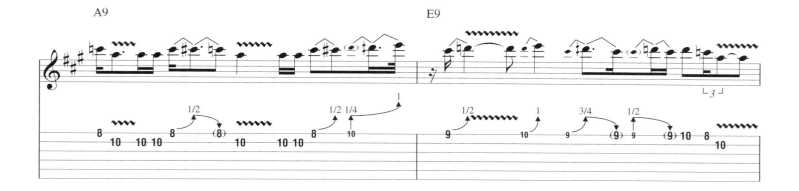

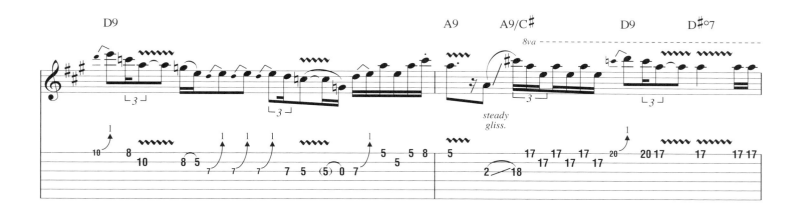

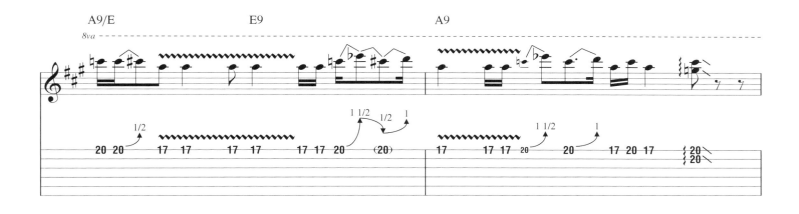

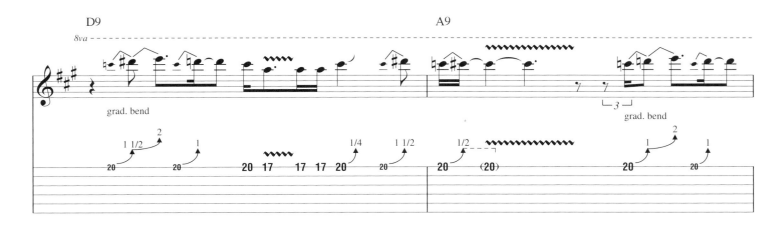

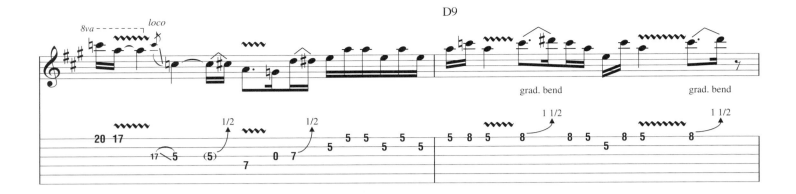

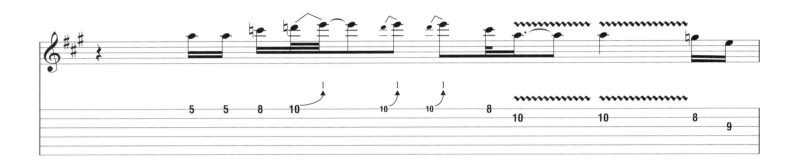

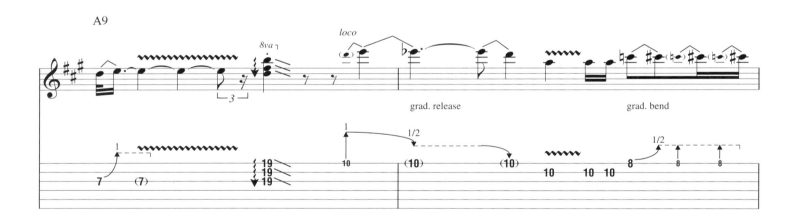

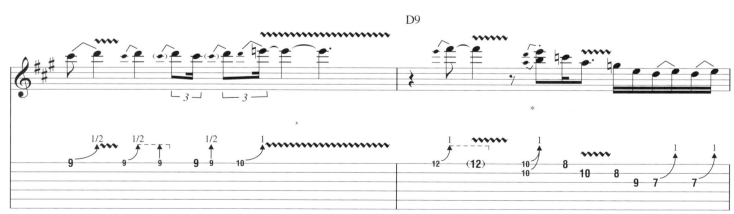

*Bend both notes w/ same finger.

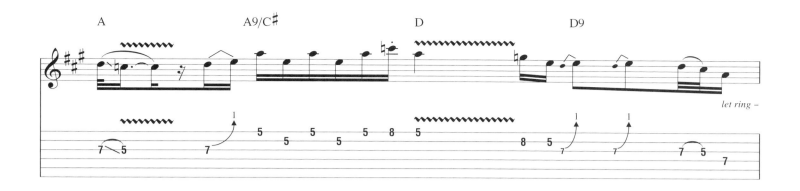

Verse

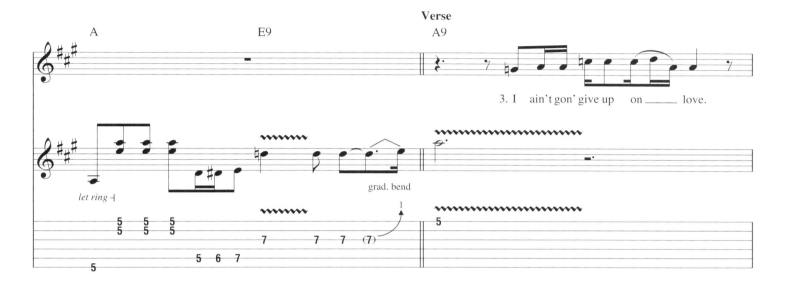

3. I ain't gon' give up on _____ love.

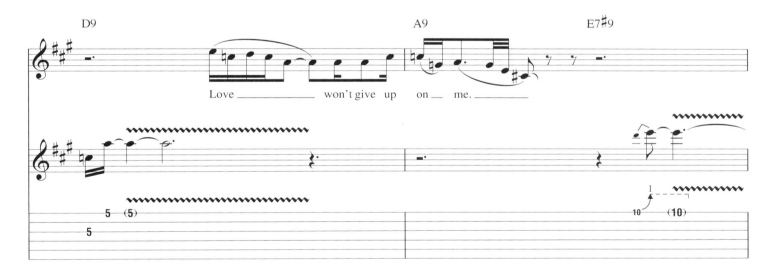

Love _____ won't give up on _ me. _____

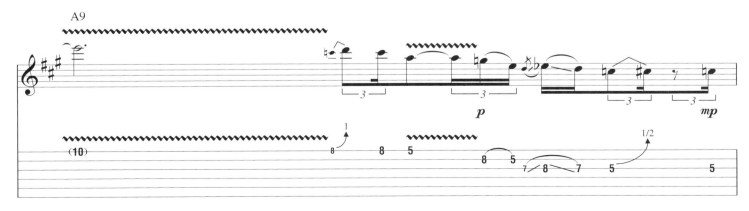

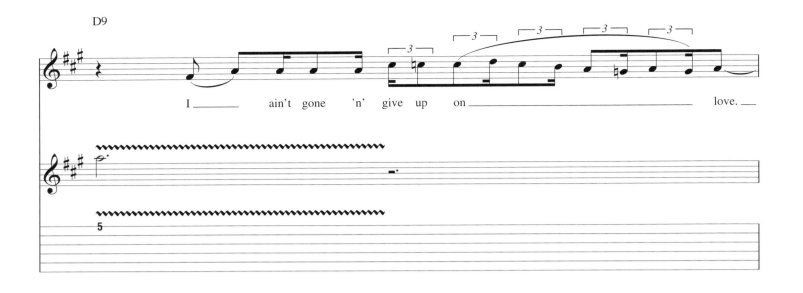

I _____ ain't gone 'n' give up on _____ love. ____

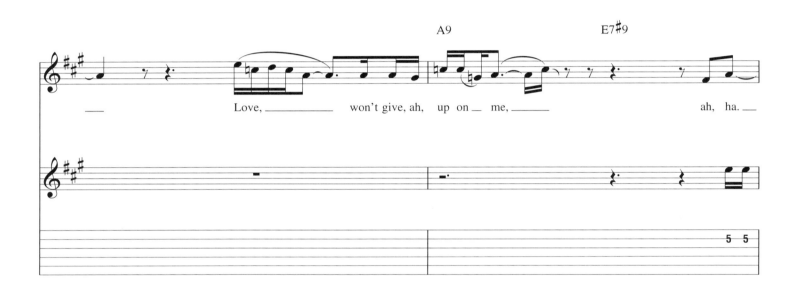

_____ Love, _____ won't give, ah, up on ___ me, _____ ah, ha. ___

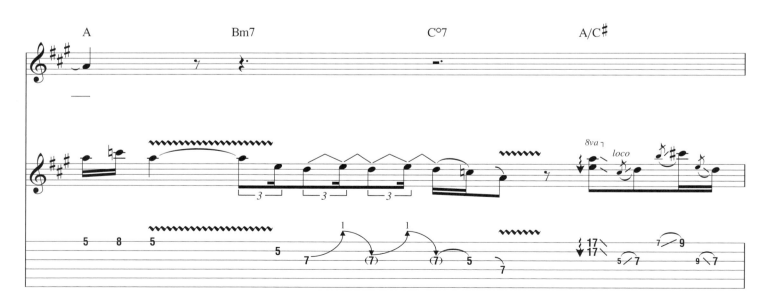

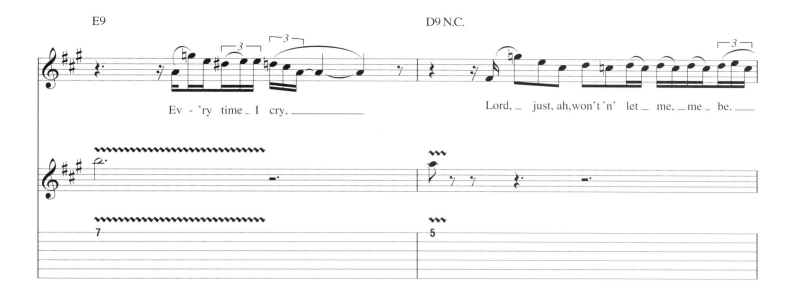

Ev - 'ry time _ I _ cry, _____

Lord, _ just, ah, won't 'n' let _ me, _ me _ be. _

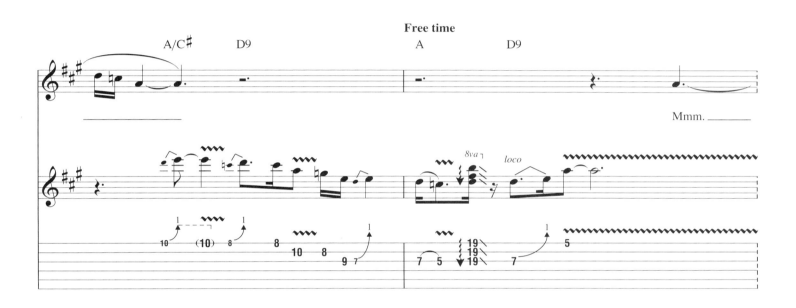

Free time

Mmm. _____

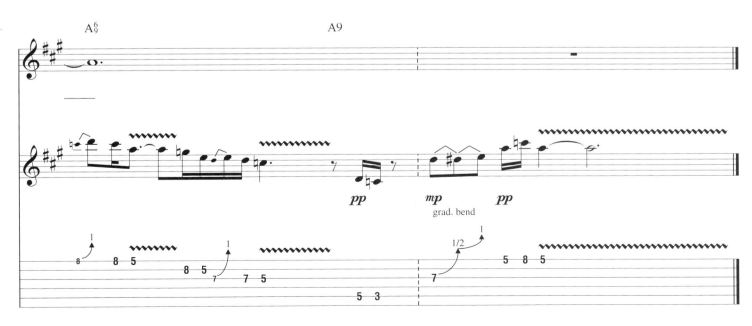

Honey Bee

Words and Music by Stevie Ray Vaughan

Tune down 1/2 step:
(low to high) E♭-A♭-D♭-G♭-B♭-E♭

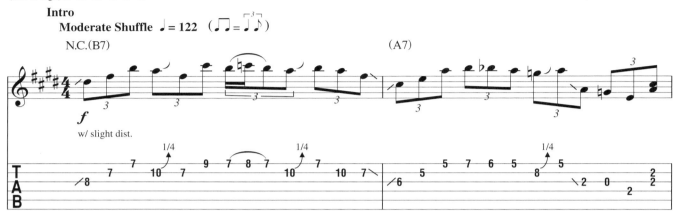

sweet as can be.   I am the king bee, ba - by,   buzz with me.

Dive in your hive ___ and in-to your life, ___ tell ___ me, lit-tle ba-by, that you'll

Bridge
A7

buzz me all the time. 'Cause the way we kiss just can't miss. ___
See additional lyrics

Don't make me wait to feel your warm em-brace. Each and ev-'ry time

To Coda

N.C.(B)

that we get the chance, ___ c-'mon, lit-tle ba-by, let's, ah, make some ro - mance.

Guitar Solo

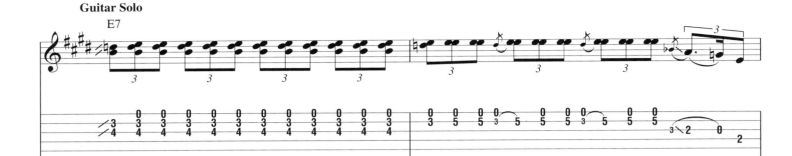

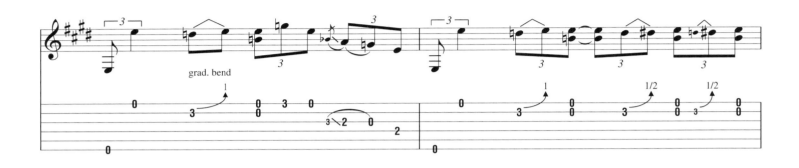

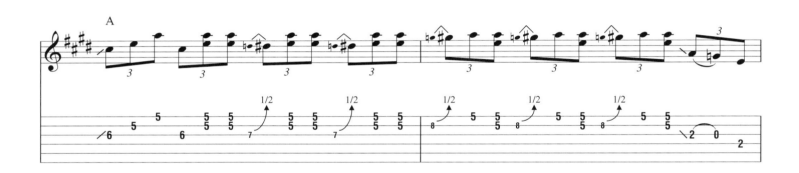

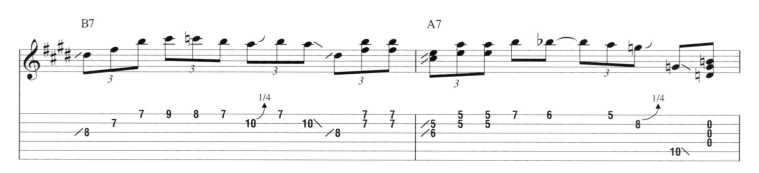

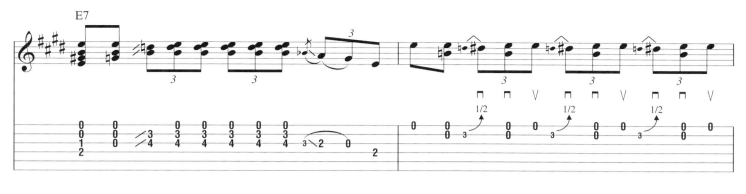

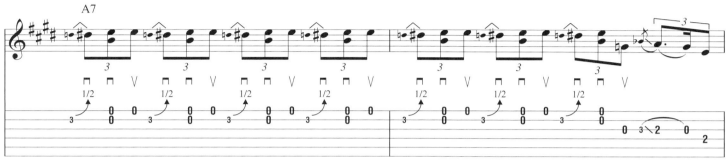

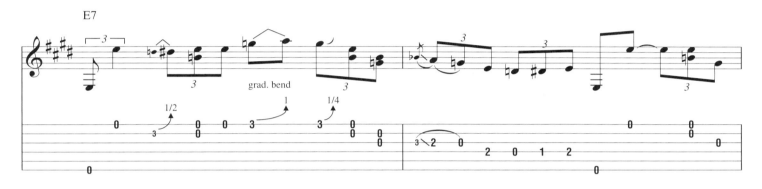

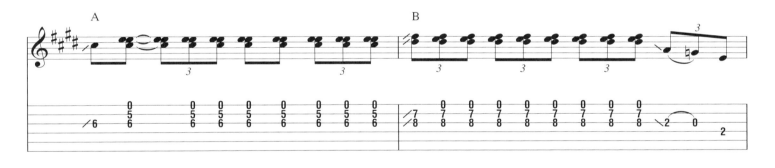

D.S. al Coda

Yeah, you

⊕ Coda

Outro-Guitar Solo

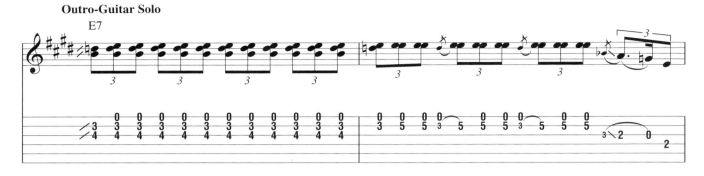

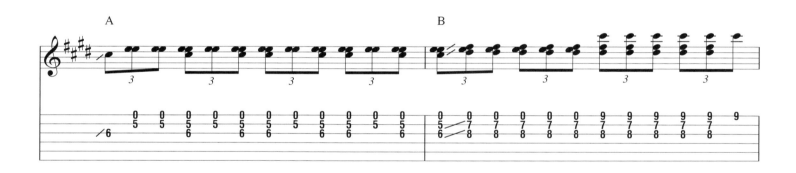

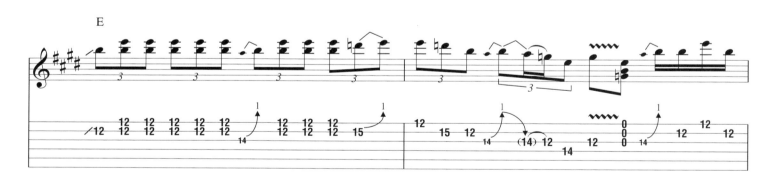

*Snap string w/ thumb.

Additional Lyrics

Bridge   Yeah, you really groove me, baby, when you move your hips.
             Shake it all around, it takes me pound for pound.
             I want you all the time just because,
             You know you really have give me a buzz.

Pride and Joy

By Stevie Ray Vaughan

Tune down 1/2 step:
(low to high) Eb-Ab-Db-Gb-Bb-Eb

Verse

1. Well, you've heard a - bout lov - in' giv - in' sight ___ to the blind. ___

My ba - by's lov - in' cause the sun ___ to shine. ___ An' she's my sweet ___ lit - tle thang, ___

she's my pride and joy. ___ She's ___ my

sweet lit - tle ba - by, I'm ___ her ___ lit - tle lov - er boy. ___

Verse

3. Yeah, I love my la-dy, to be long and __ lean. __

You mess with her, you'll see a man get-tin' mean. __ She's my sweet __ lit-tle thang, __

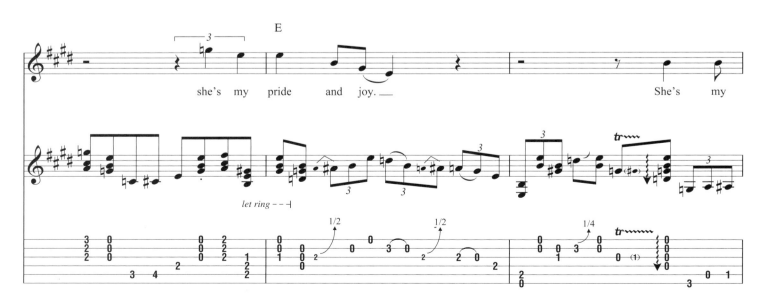

she's my pride and joy. __ She's my

sweet ___ lit - tle ba - by, I'm ___ her ___ lit - tle lov - er boy. ___

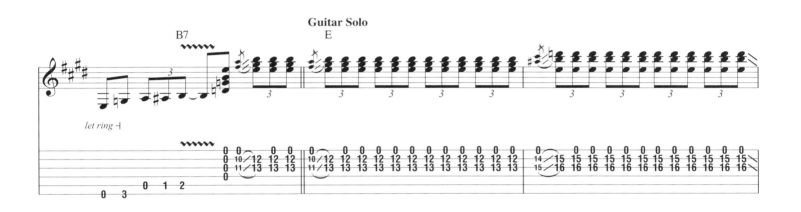

Guitar Solo

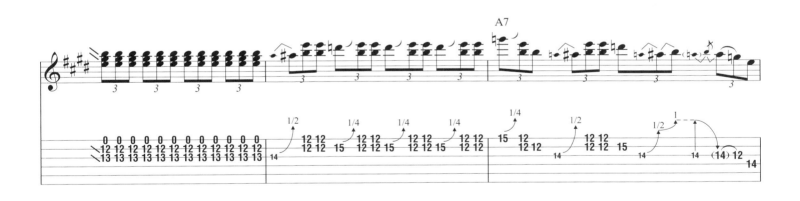

4. Well, I love my ba - by, like the fin - est w - wine. _

Love like ___ ours, ah, won't ___ nev - er grow ___ old. ___ She's my sweet ___ lit - tle thang, ___

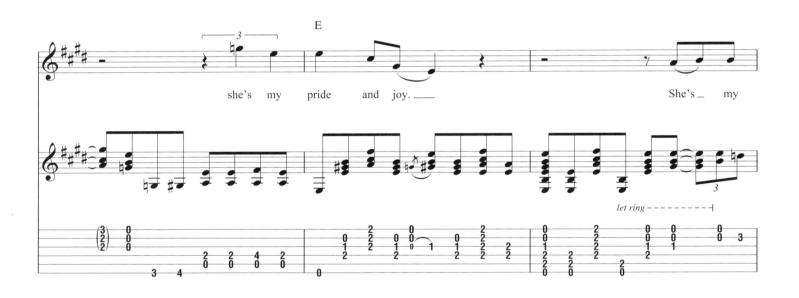

she's my pride and joy. ___ She's ___ my

sweet lit-tle ba - by, I'm ___ her lit - tle lov - er boy. ___

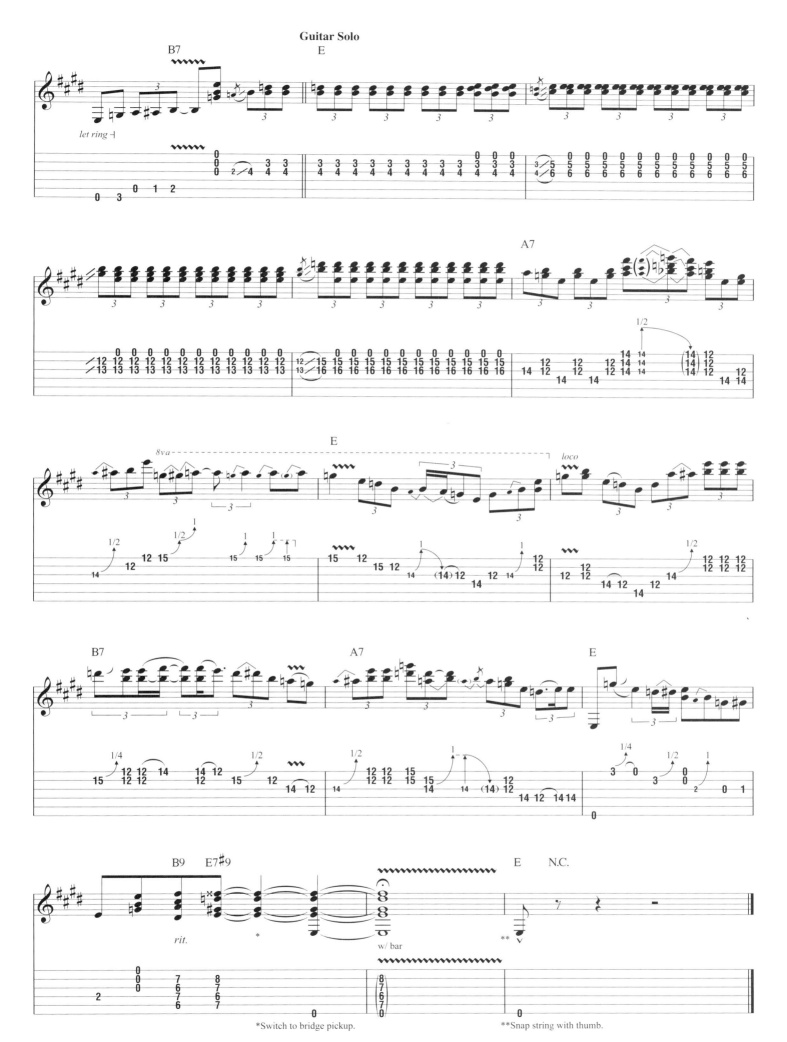

*Switch to bridge pickup.   **Snap string with thumb.

Rude Mood

Music by Stevie Ray Vaughan

Tune down 1/2 step:
(low to high) E♭-A♭-D♭-G♭-B♭-E♭

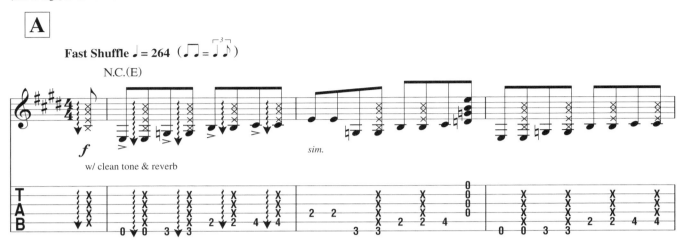

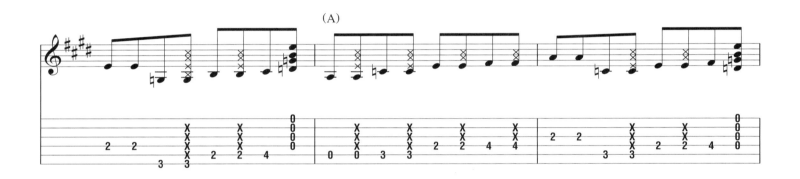

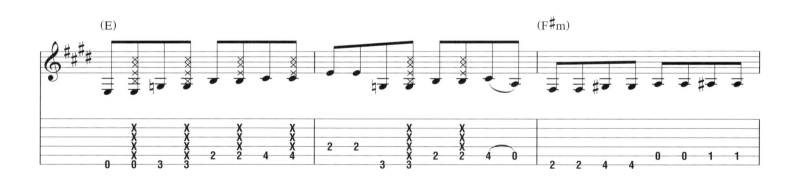

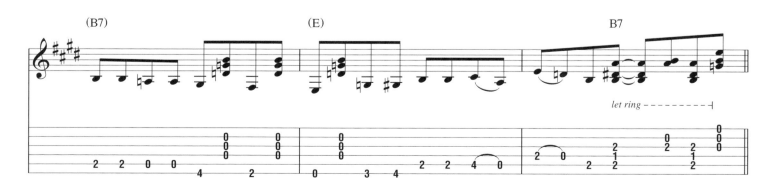

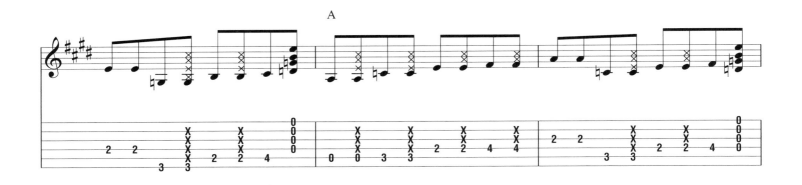

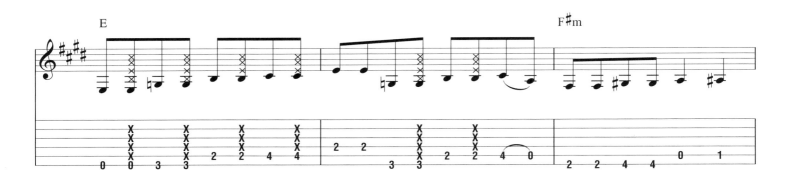

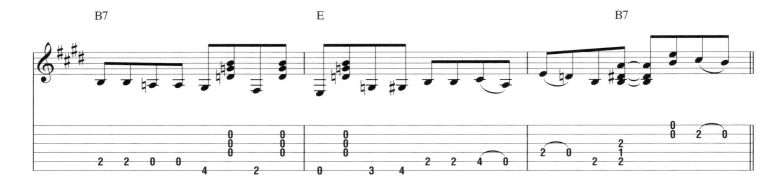

D

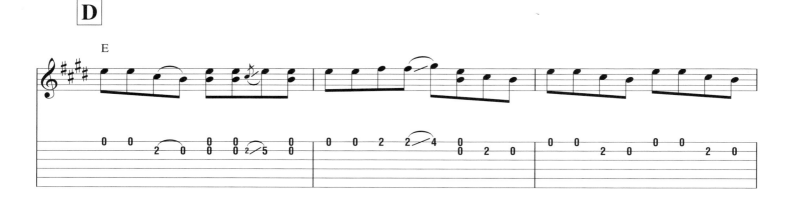

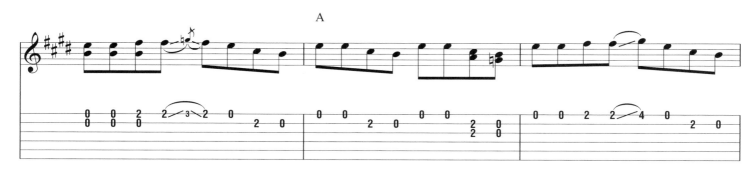

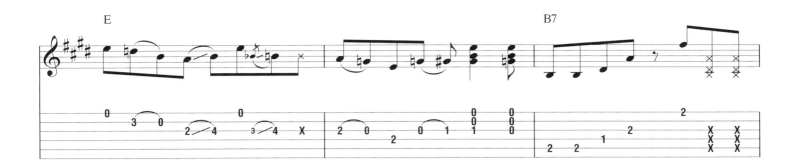

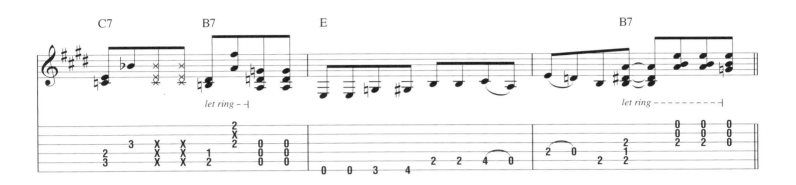

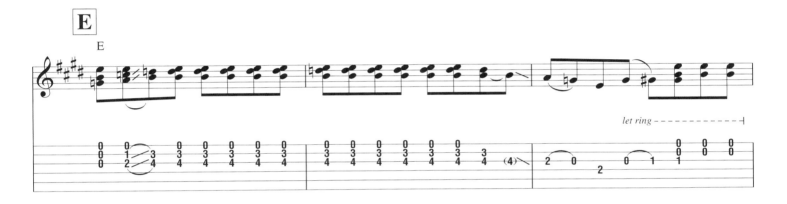

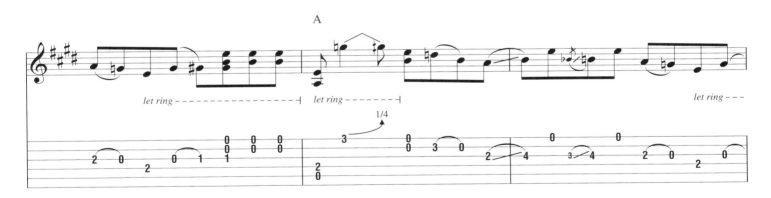

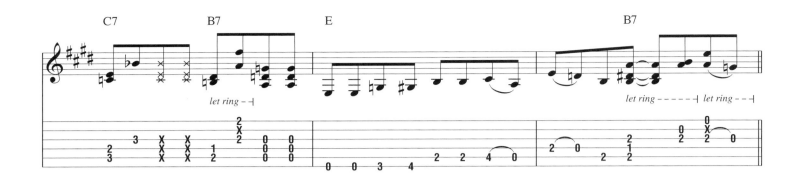

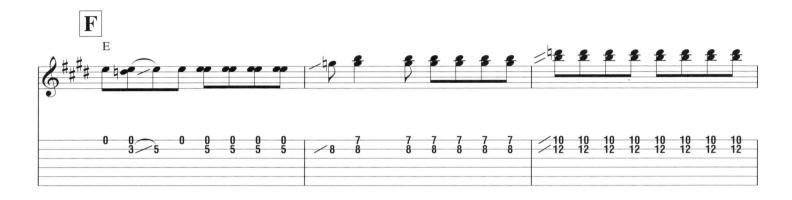

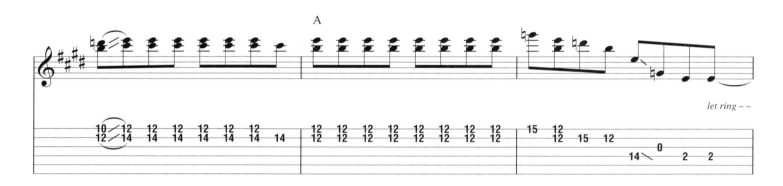

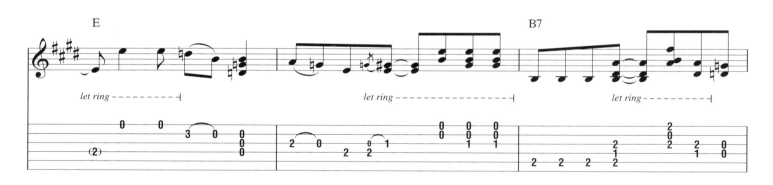

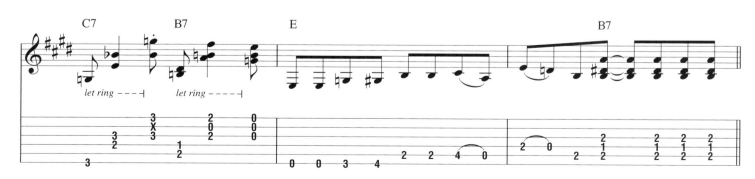

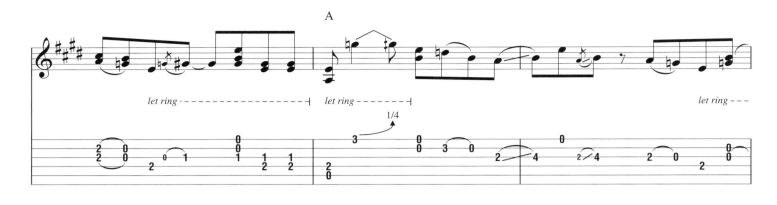

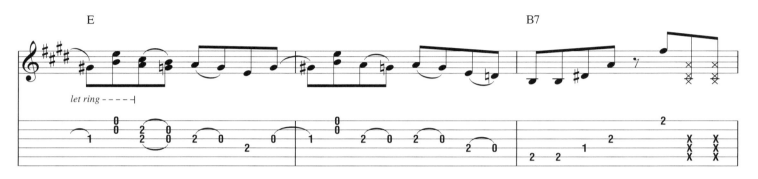

I

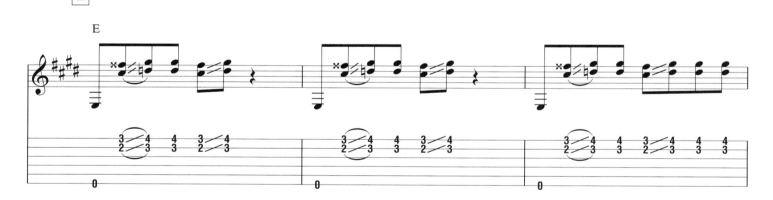

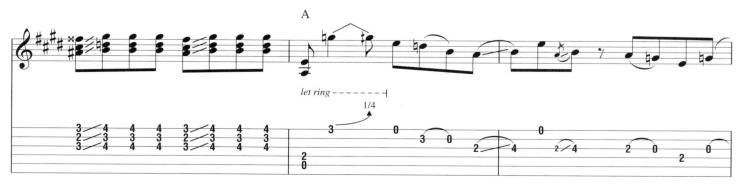

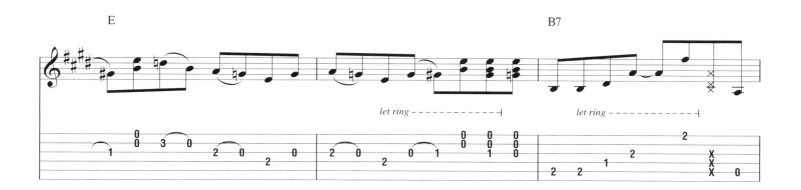

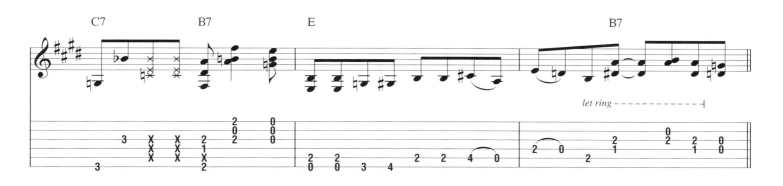

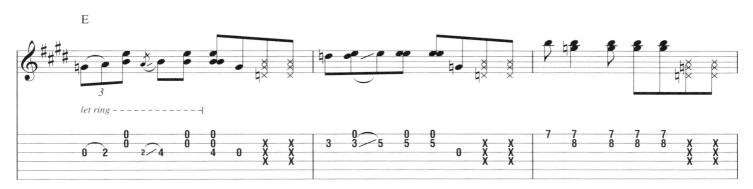

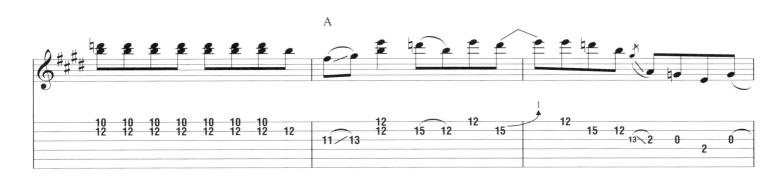

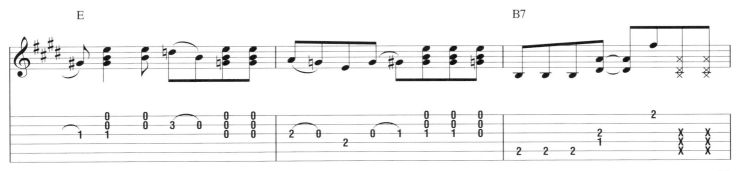

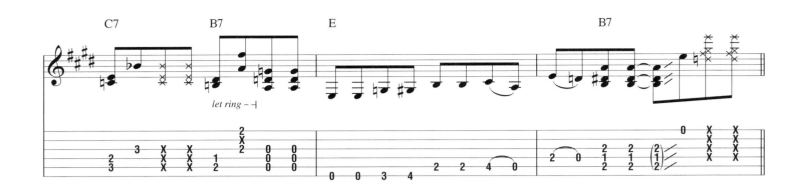

K

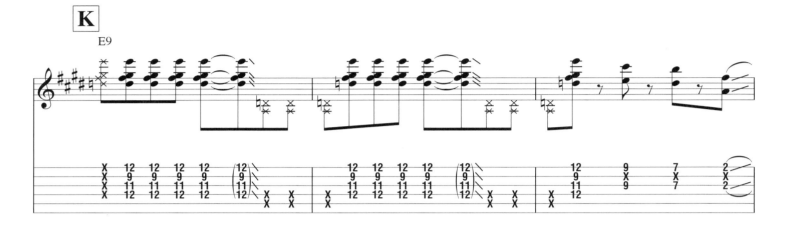

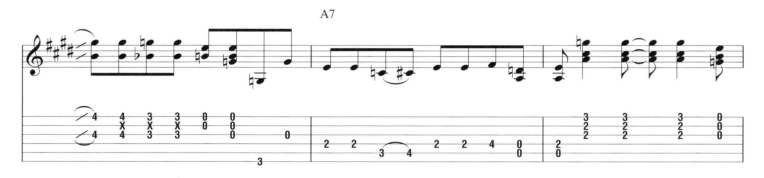

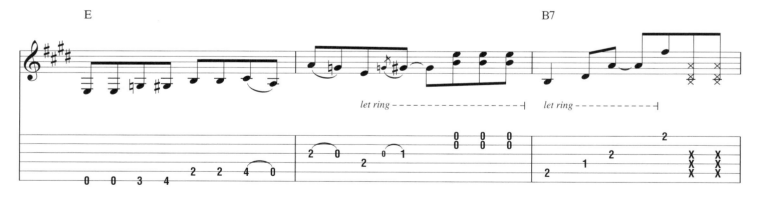

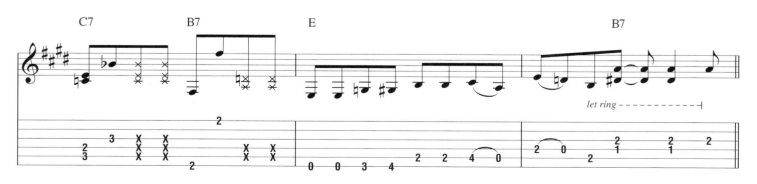

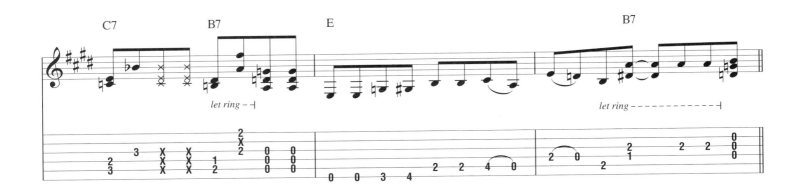

P

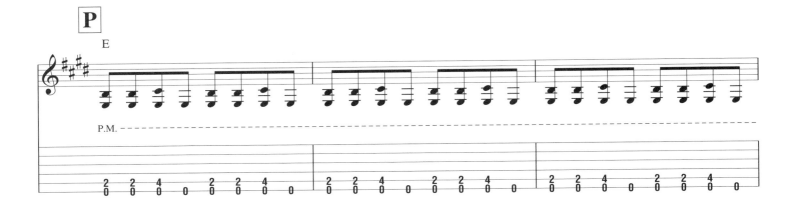

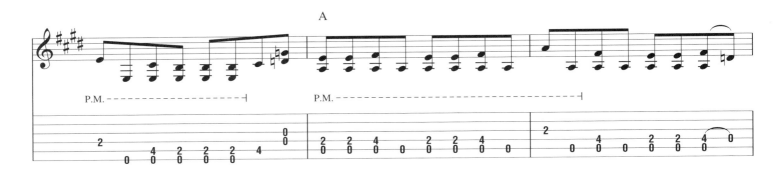

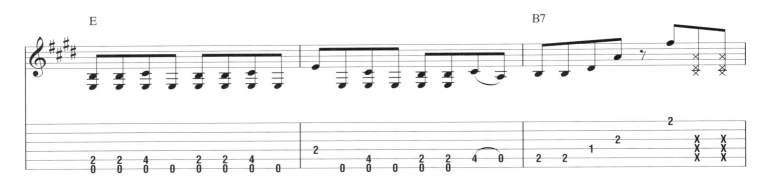

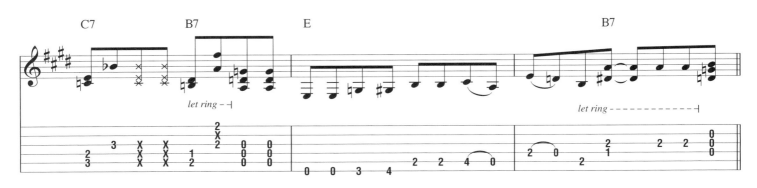

A

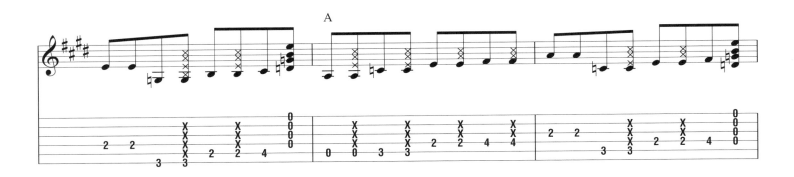

E   F#m

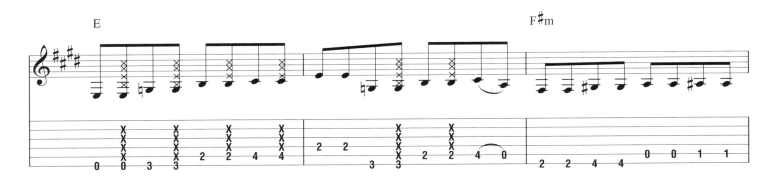

B7   E   B7

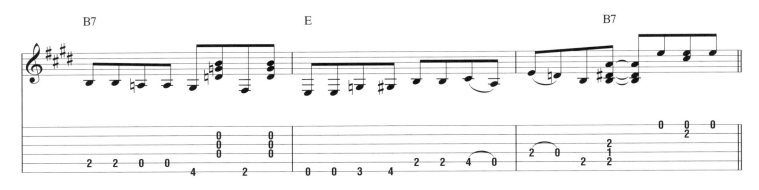

S

E

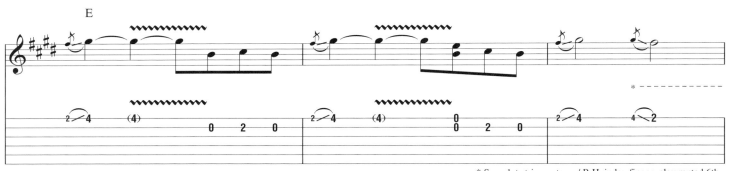

* Snap 1st string notes w/ R.H. index finger, play muted 6th
string notes w/ R.H. thumb slap.

A

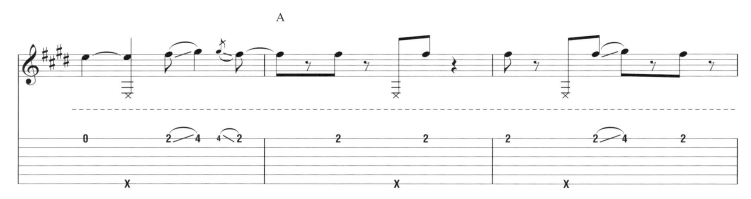

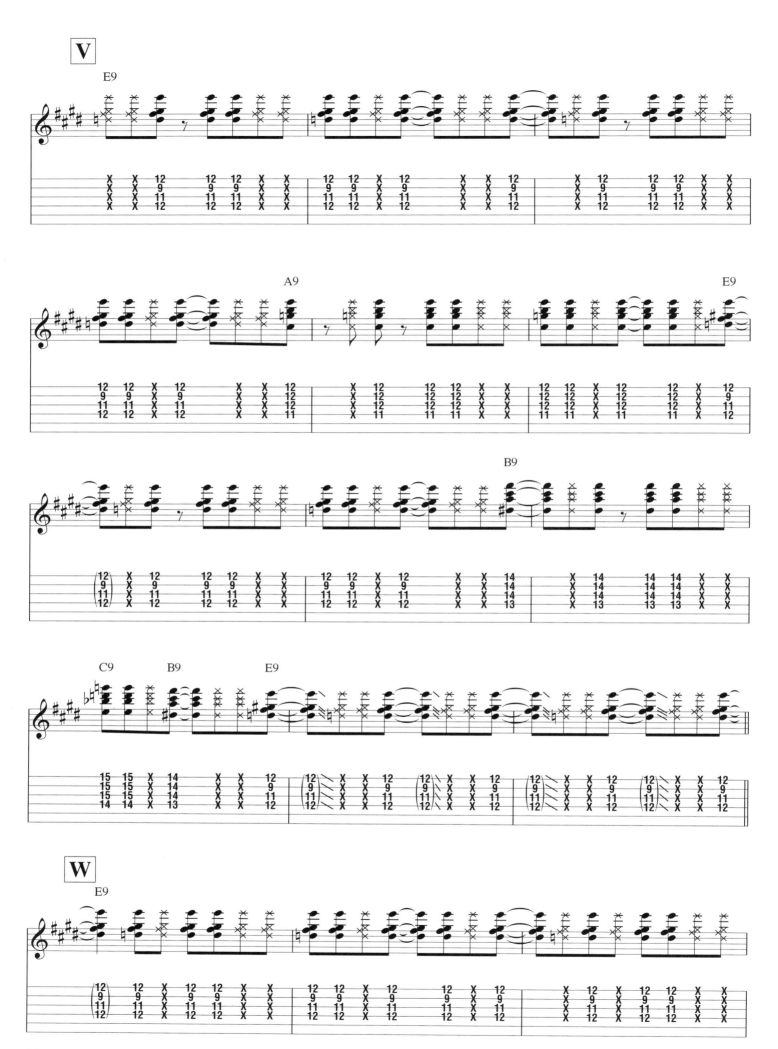

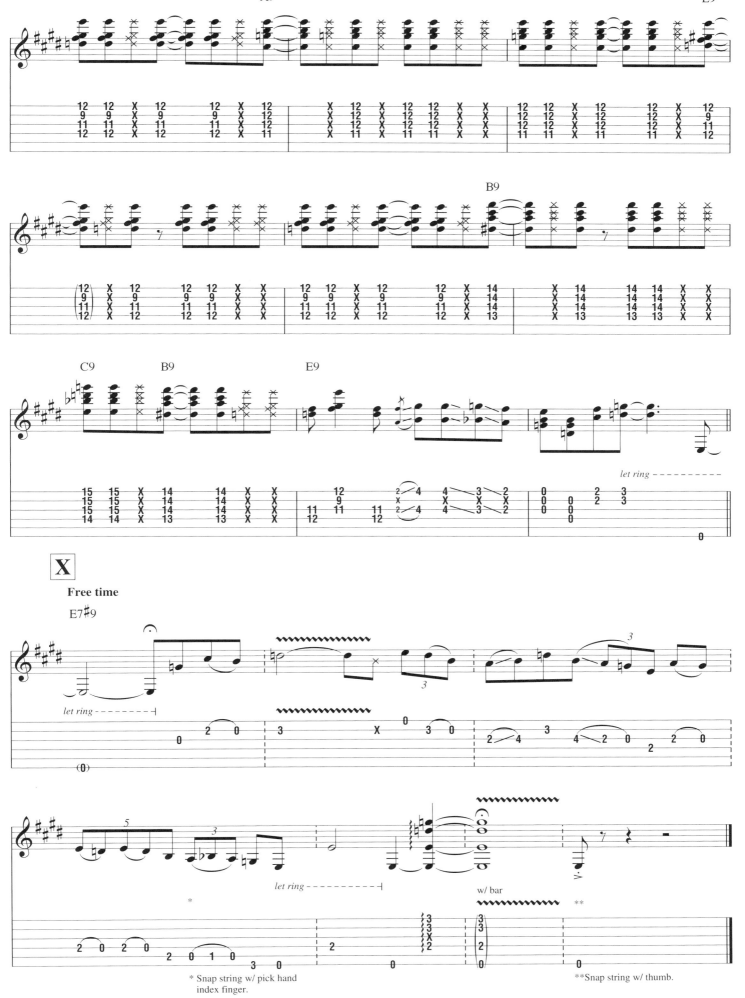

* Snap string w/ pick hand
  index finger.

**Snap string w/ thumb.

Texas Flood

Words and Music by Larry Davis and Joseph W. Scott

Tune down 1/2 step:
(low to high) E♭-A♭-D♭-G♭-B♭-E♭

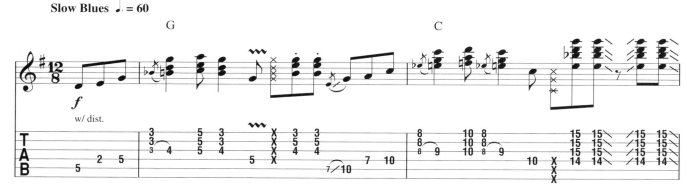

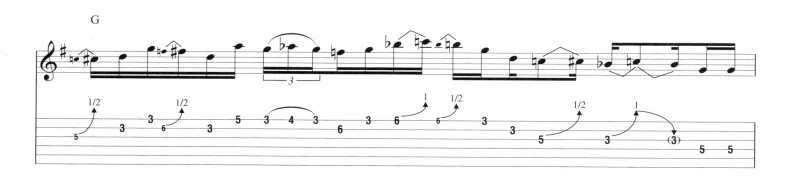

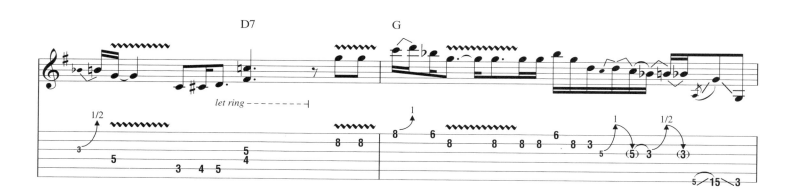

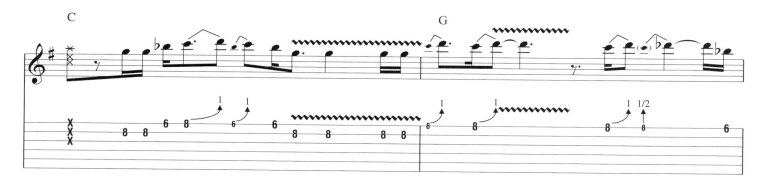

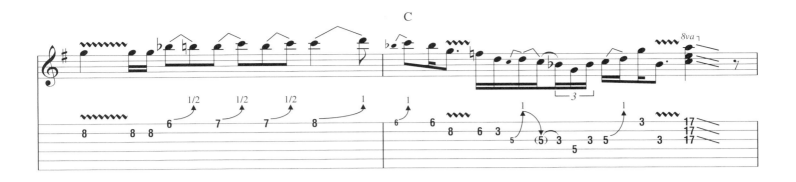

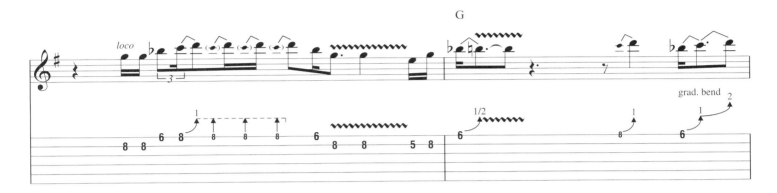

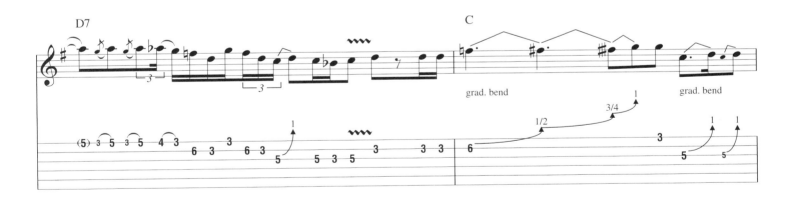

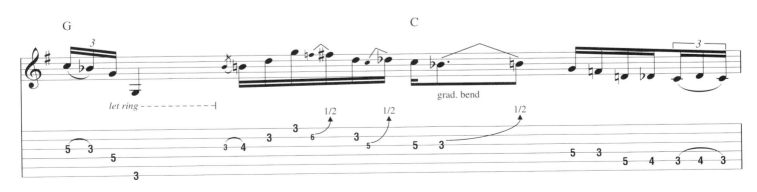

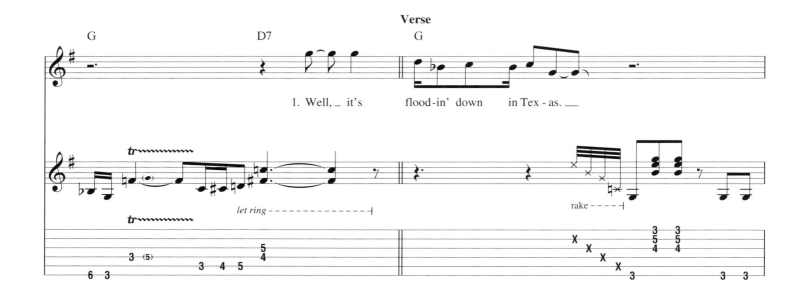

1. Well, _ it's   flood-in' down   in Tex - as. _

All of the tel - e - phone lines _ are down. _

Well, _____ it's _

flood-in' down ___ in Tex-as. ___   All ___ of the tel-e-phone lines ___ are down. _

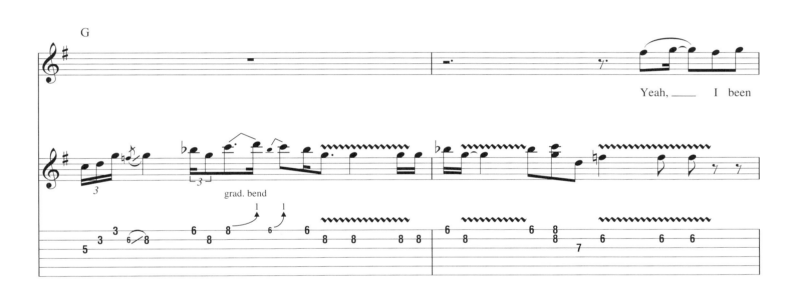

Yeah, ___ I been

try-in' to call ___ my ba-by. ___   Lord, ___ 'n' I can't ___ get a sin - gle sound. _

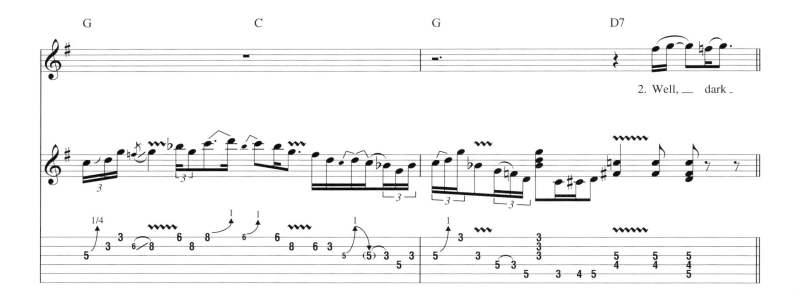

2. Well, ___ dark ___

Verse

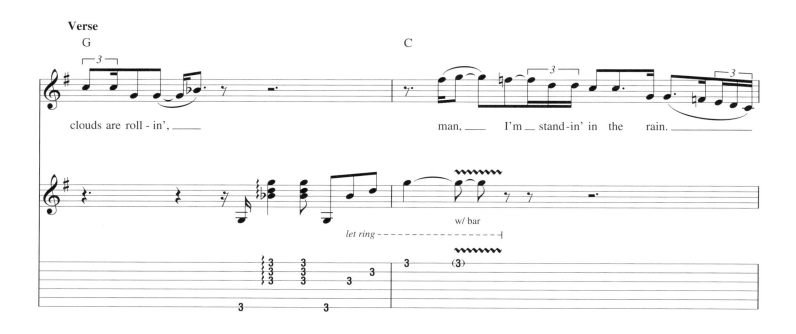

clouds are roll - in', ___ man, ___ I'm ___ stand - in' in the rain. ___

let ring

w/ bar

Well, ___ dark ___

56

clouds are roll-in', _____

man, _____ an' I'm stand-in' out in ___ the rain. _____

Yeah, _____ flood _____

wa-ter keep a roll - in', _

man, it's a-bout to drive poor me in - sane. _

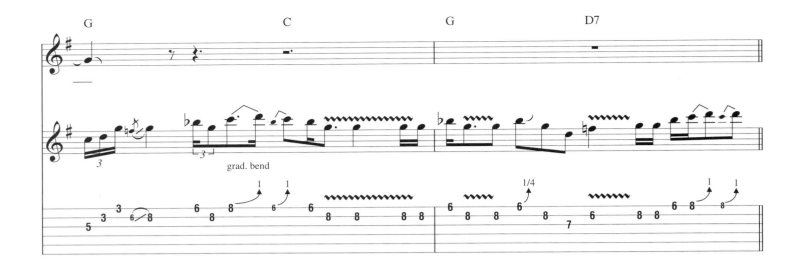

Guitar Solo

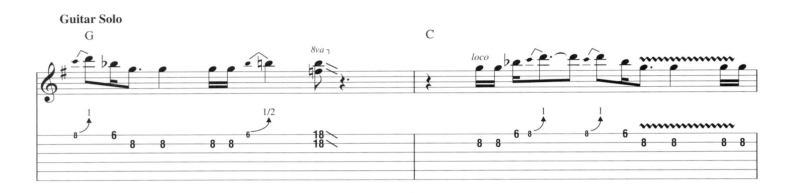

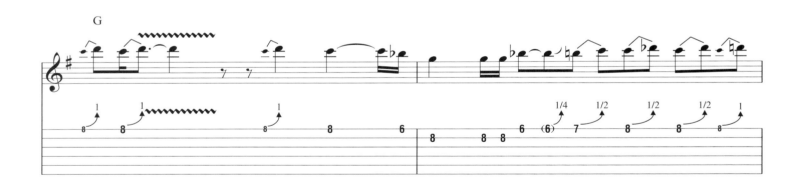

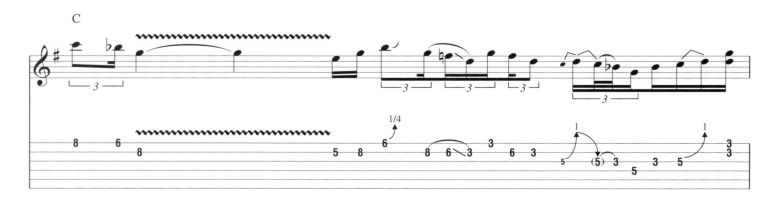

G

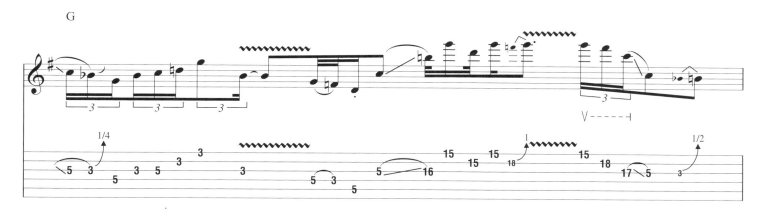

D7

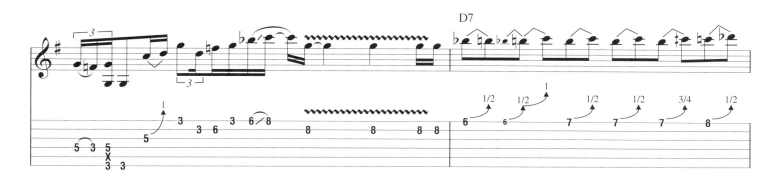

C   G   C

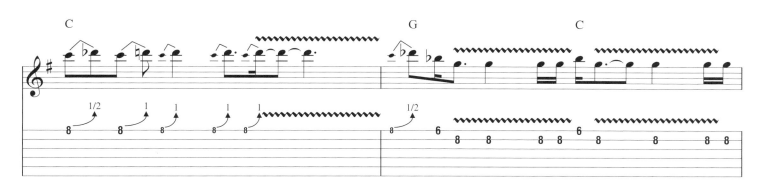

G   D7   G

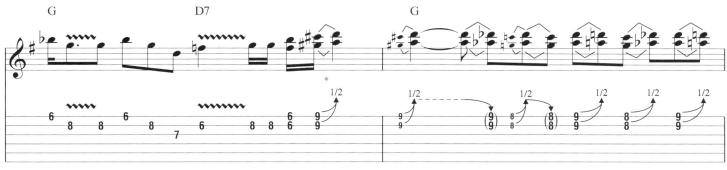

*Bend both strings w/ same finger, next 2 meas.

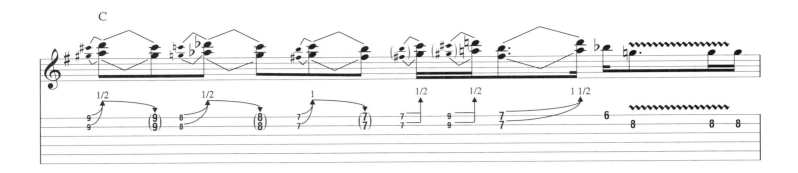

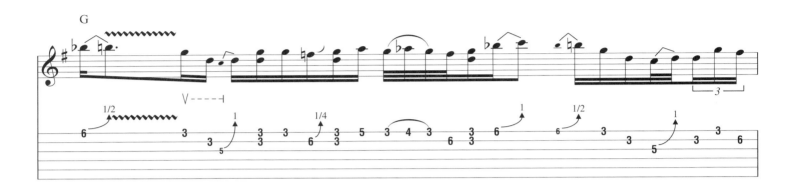

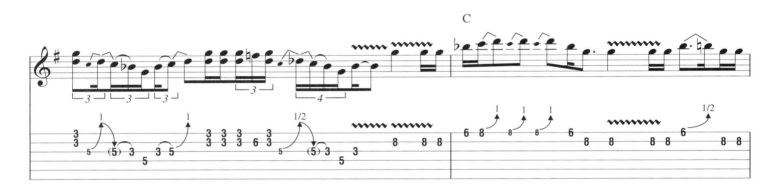

*As before, this measure only.

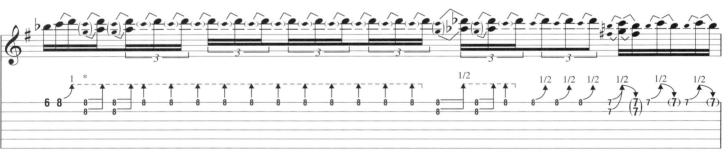

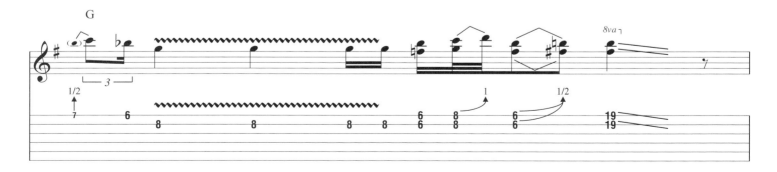

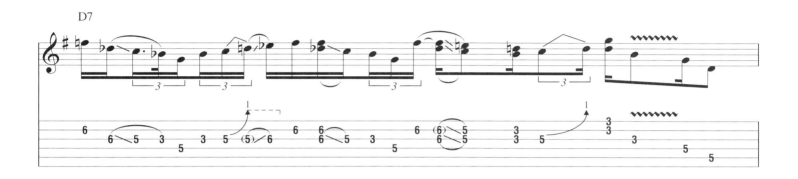

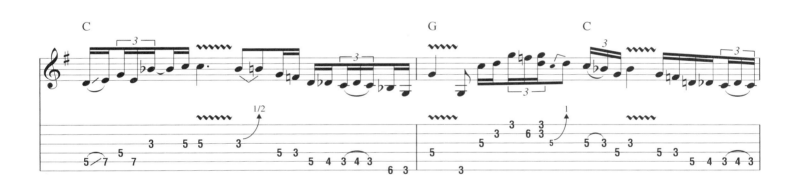

3. Well, __ I'm leav-in' you, ba - by. _____

Lord, ___ now I'm go - in' back home ___ to stay.

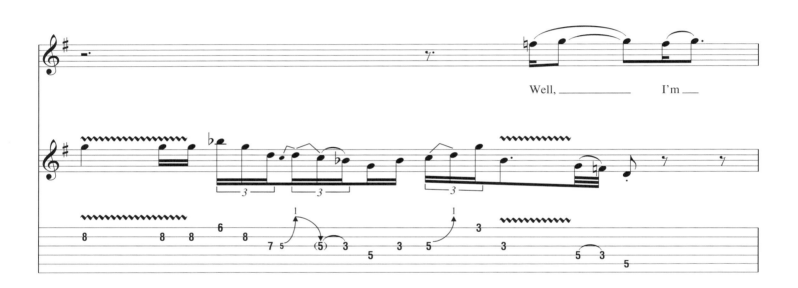

Well, _____ I'm ___

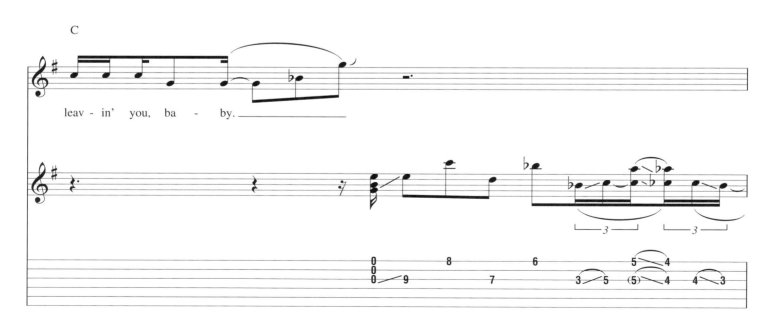

leav - in' you, ba - by. _____

Lord, _____ 'n' I'm go - in' back home to stay.

G

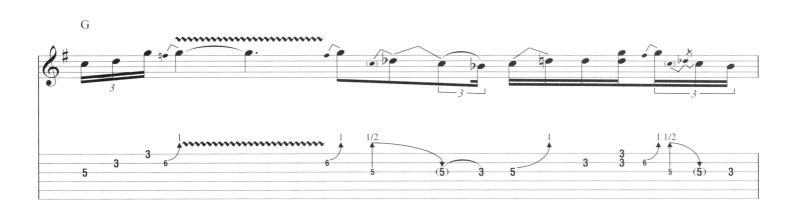

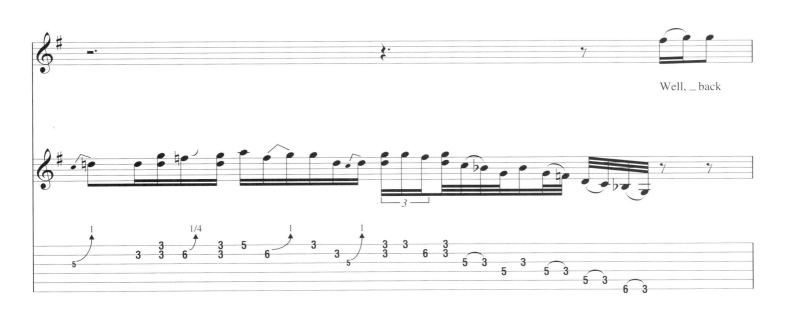

Well, _ back

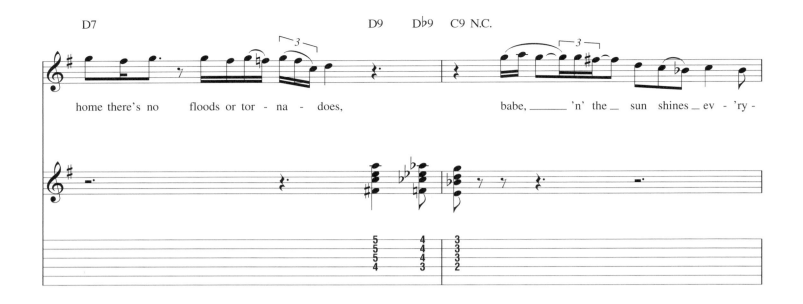

home there's no   floods or tor - na - does,   babe, _____ 'n' the __ sun shines __ ev - 'ry -

Free time

day. _____

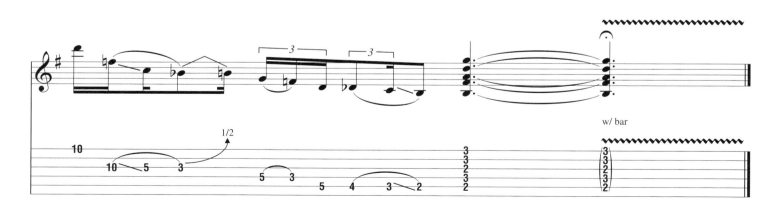

w/ bar

Voodoo Child (Slight Return)

Words and Music by Jimi Hendrix

Intro

Moderately slow ♩ = 94

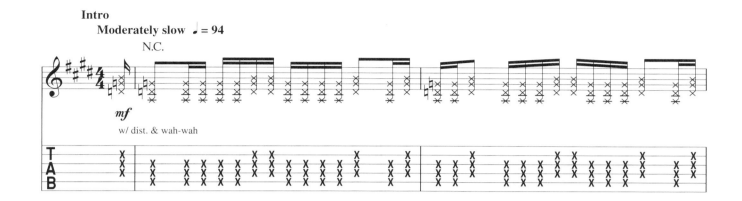

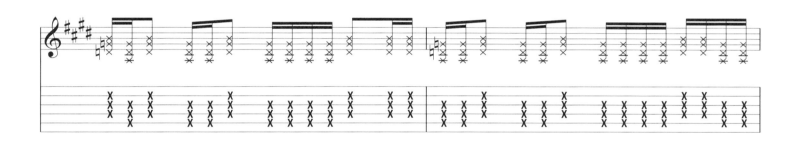

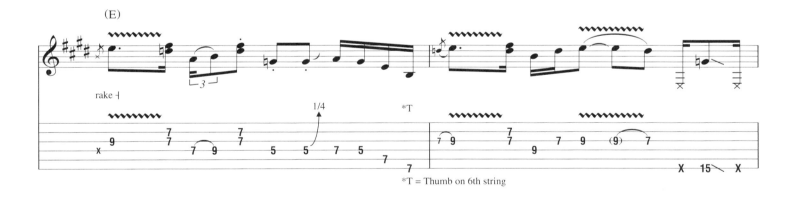

*T = Thumb on 6th string

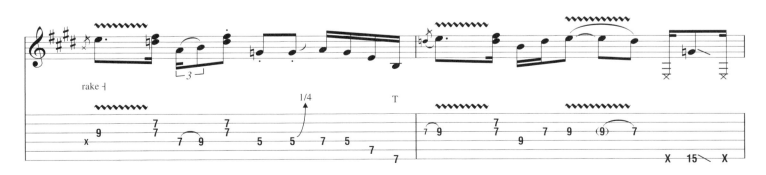

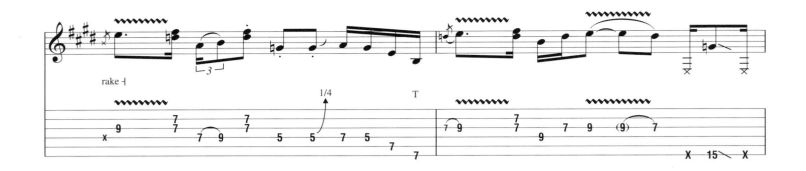

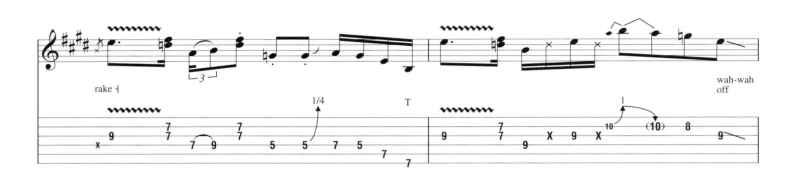

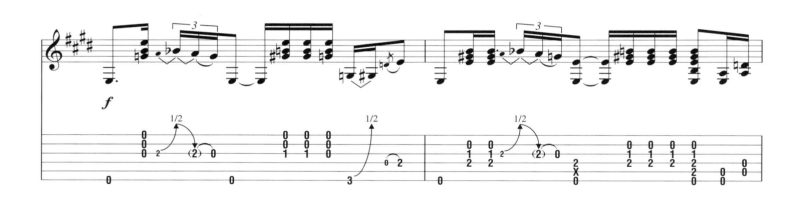

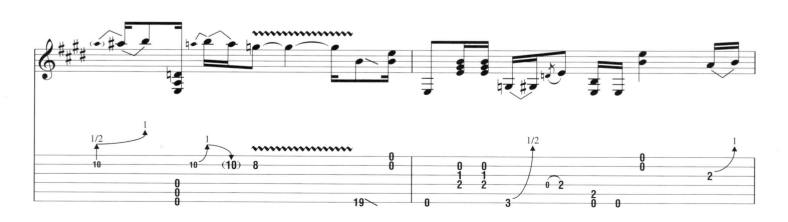

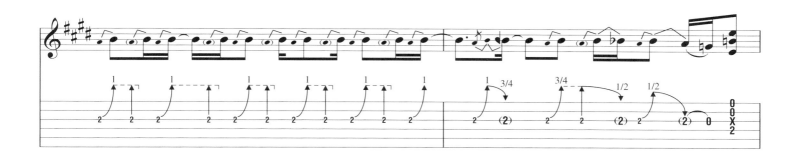

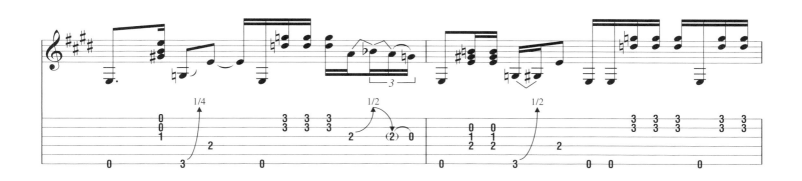

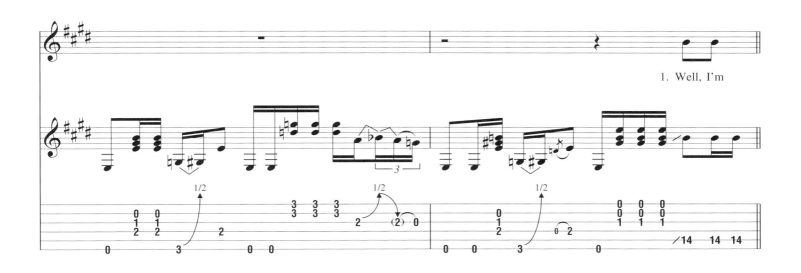

1. Well, I'm

Verse

E

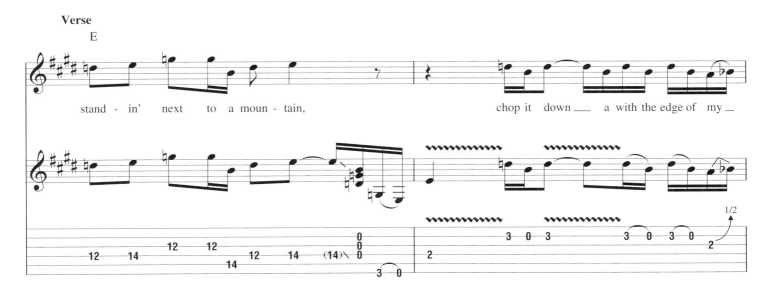

stand - in' next to a moun - tain, chop it down ___ a with the edge of my ___

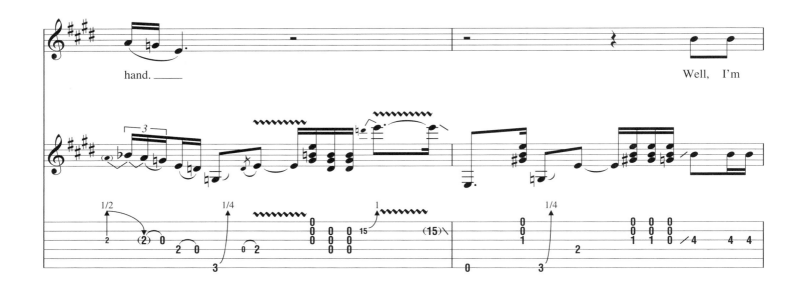

hand. _____   Well, I'm

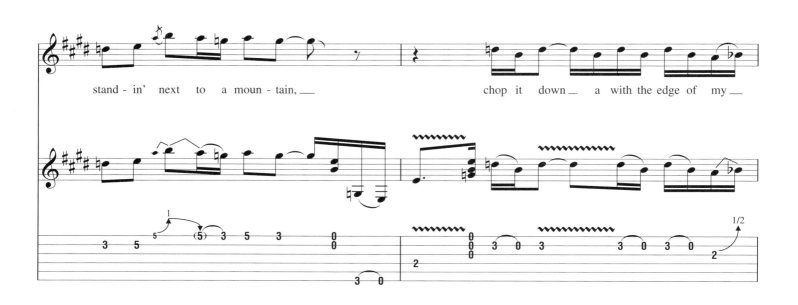

stand - in' next to a moun - tain, ___   chop it down ___ a with the edge of my ___

hand. _____

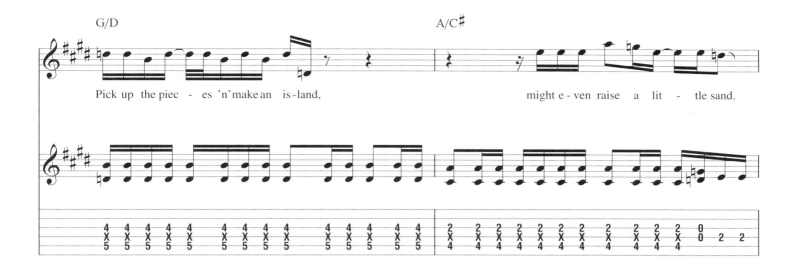

Pick up the piec - es 'n' make an is -land,   might e - ven raise a lit - tle sand.

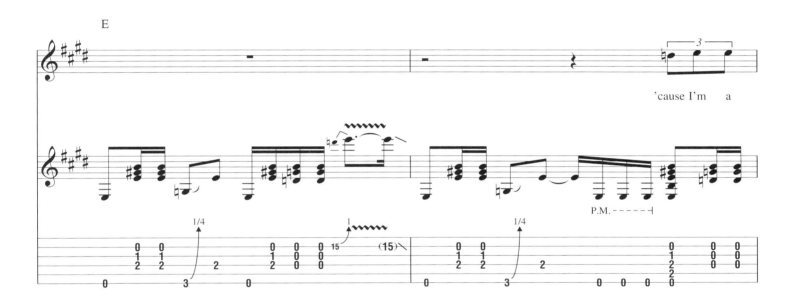

'cause I'm a

voo-doo chile, __ yeah, _____   Lord   knows, I'm a

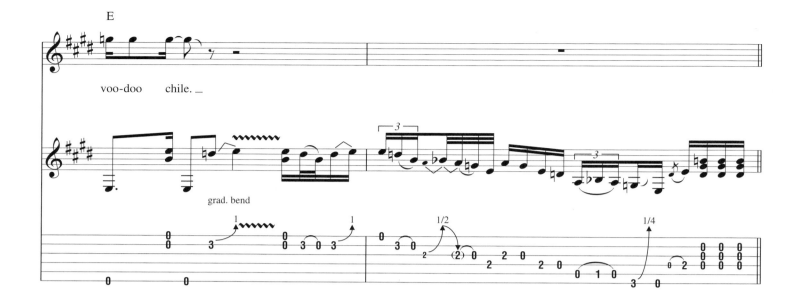

voo-doo chile. _

Guitar Solo

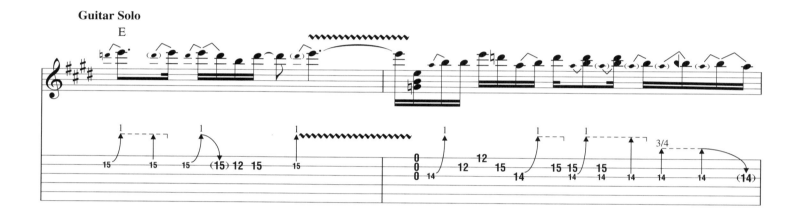

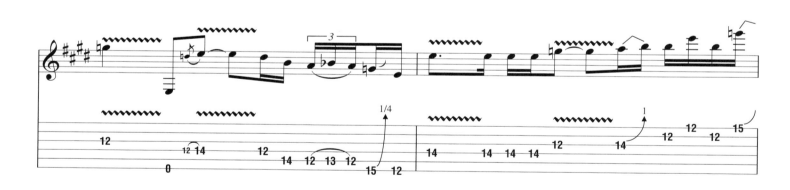

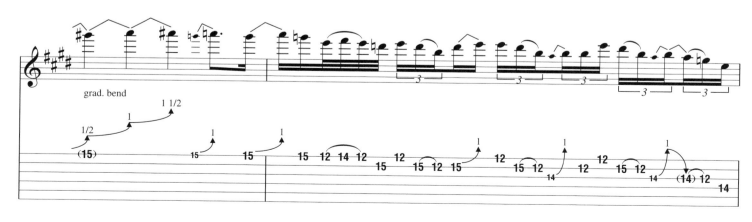

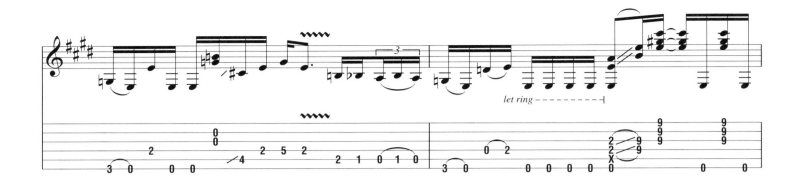

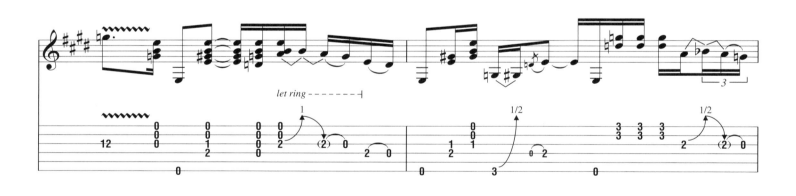

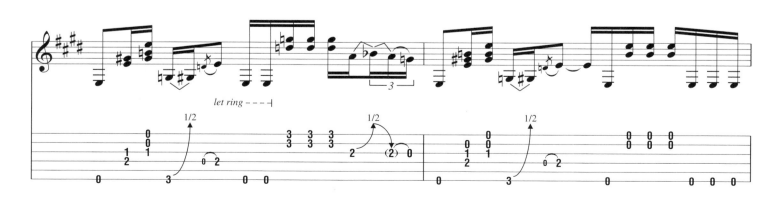

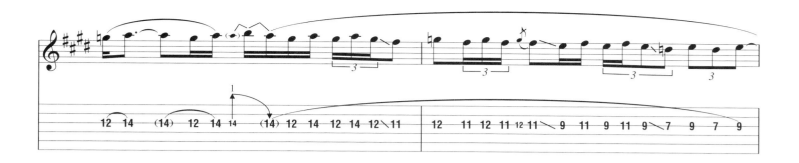

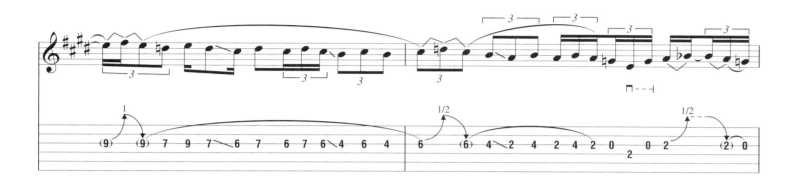

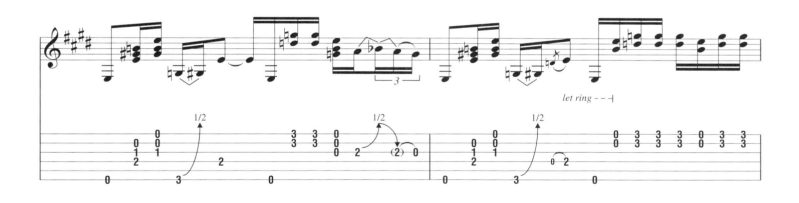

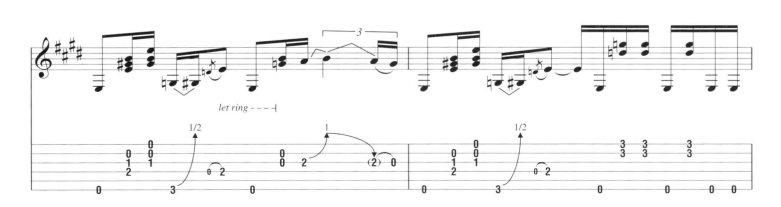

Double-time feel

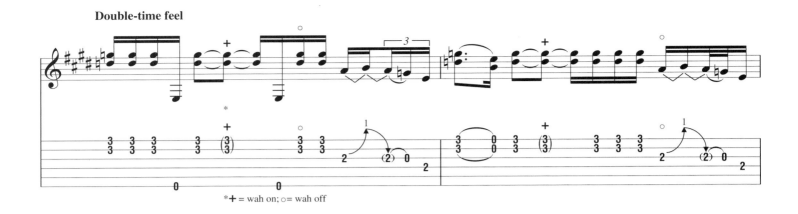

*+ = wah on; ○ = wah off

End double-time feel

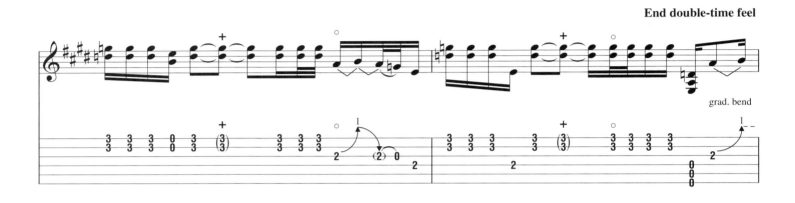

grad. bend

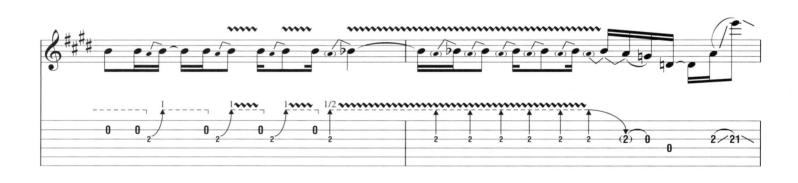

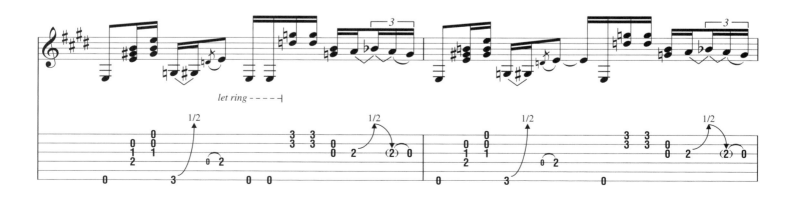

let ring - - - - ┐

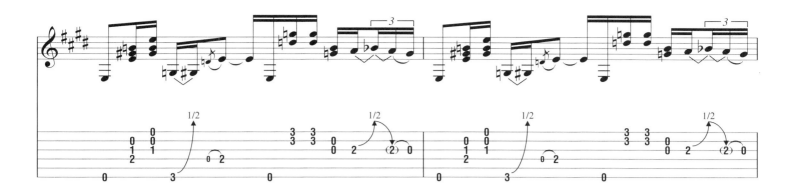

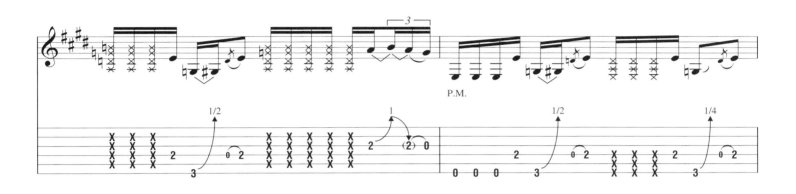

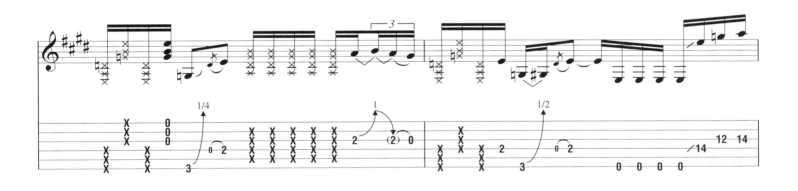

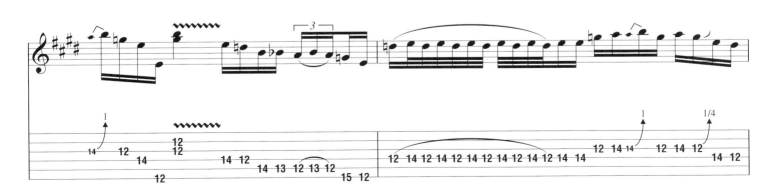

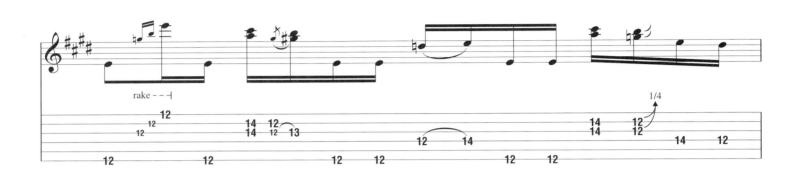

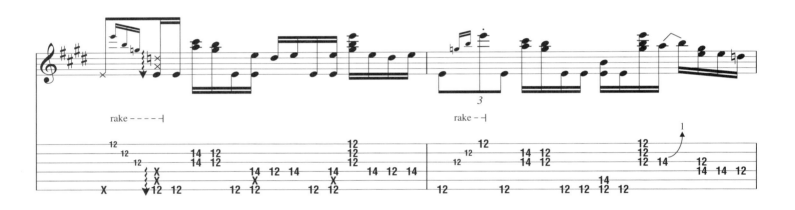

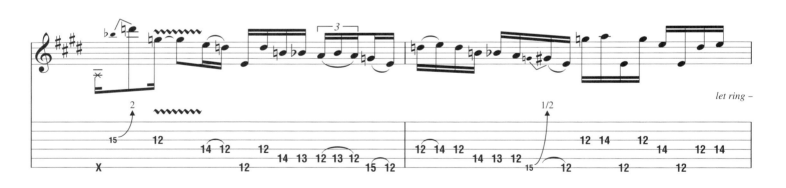

Verse

2. I did-n't mean to take up all your _____ sweet time, _

I'll give it right back to ya, a, one o' these days. _

77

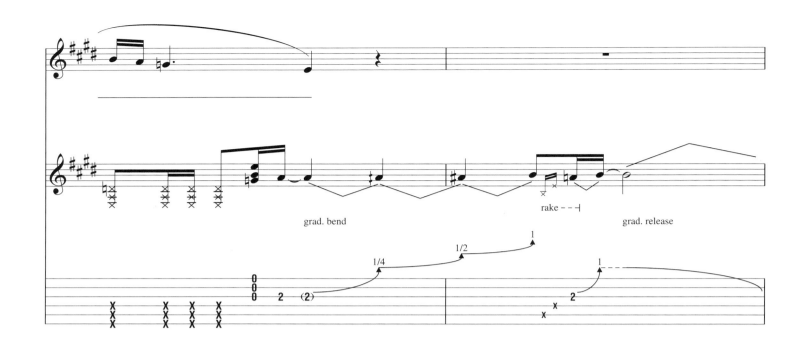

grad. bend   rake – –⌐   grad. release

rake – ⌐

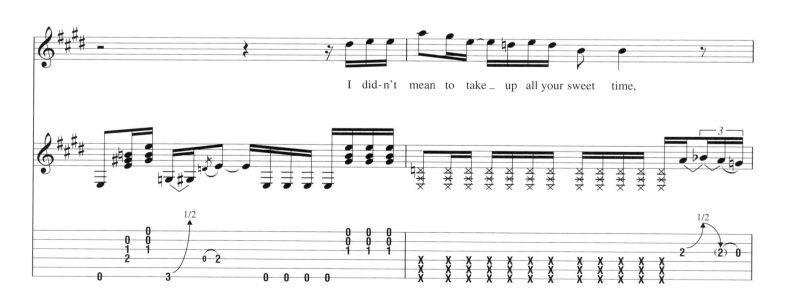

I did-n't mean to take _ up all your sweet   time,

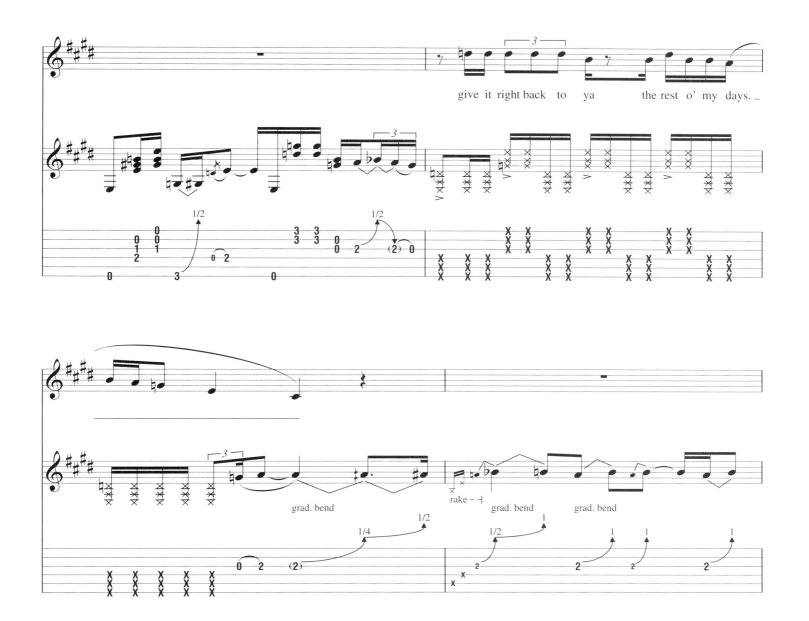

give it right back to ya the rest o' my days. _

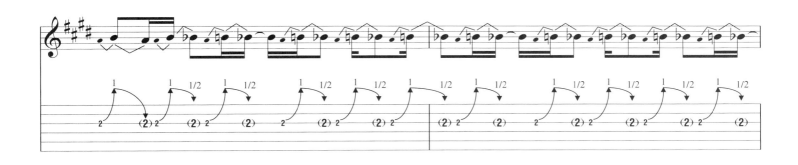

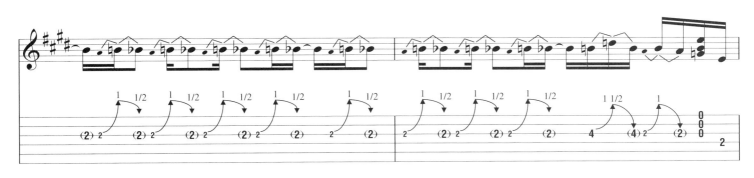

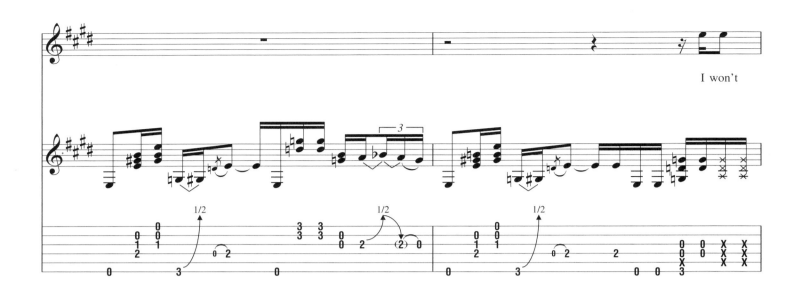

I won't

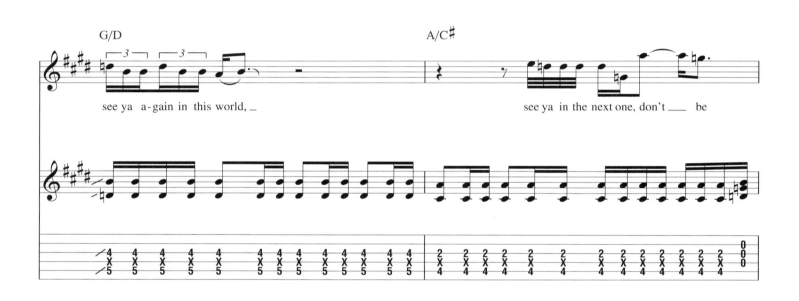

G/D

see ya a-gain in this world, __

A/C♯

see ya in the next one, don't __ be

late!

Don't __ be _____ late!

'Cause I'm a

voo-doo chile,_ yeah,_____ Lord knows I'm a

voo-doo chile._

Guitar Solo

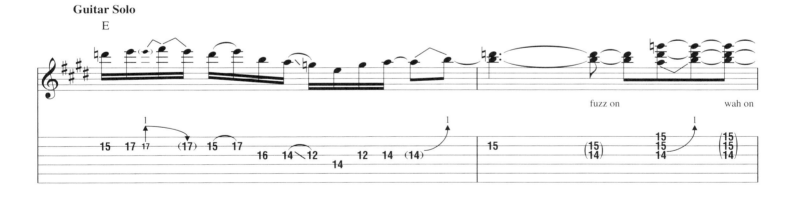

fuzz on   wah on

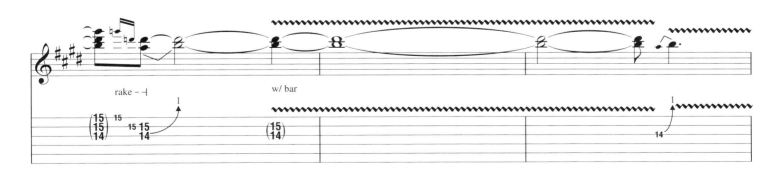

rake   w/ bar

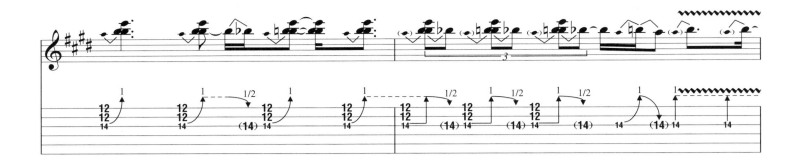

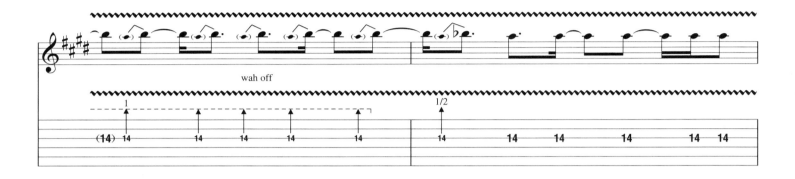

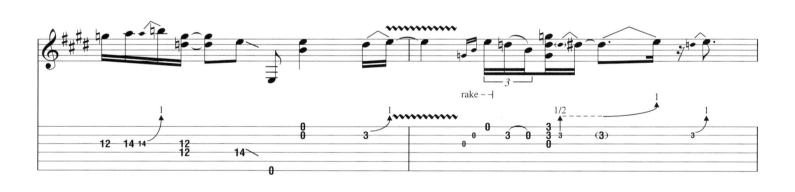

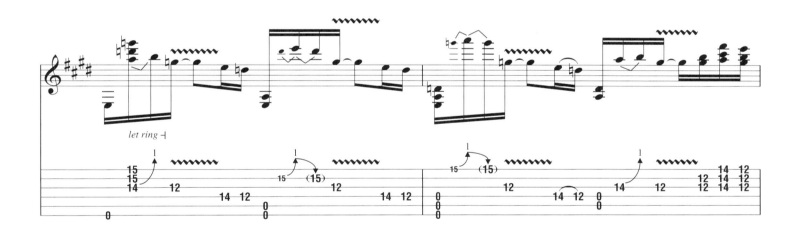

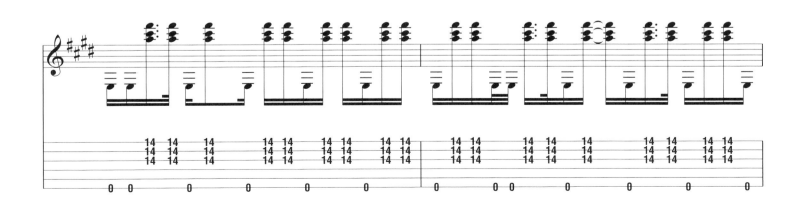

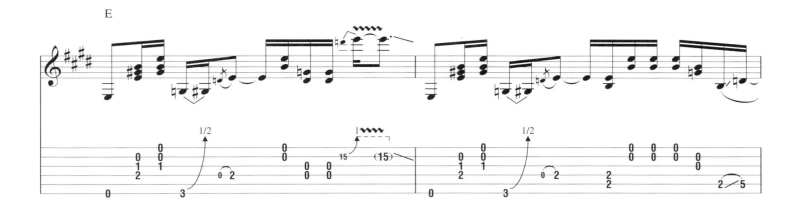

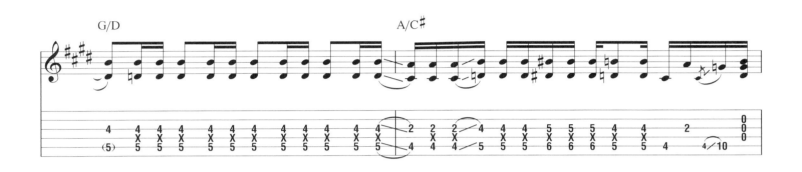

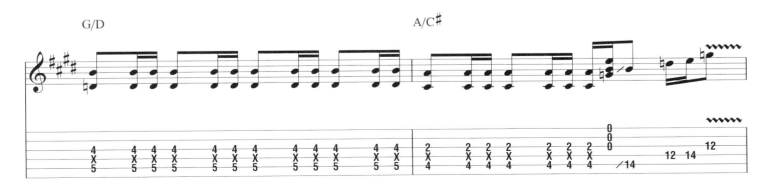

E

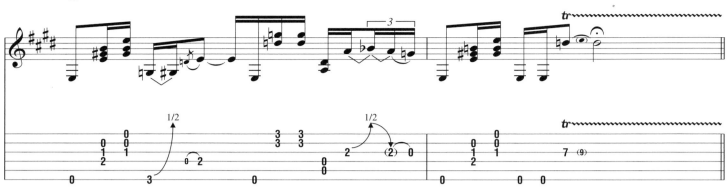

Outro
Slower ♩ = 83

N.C.(E)

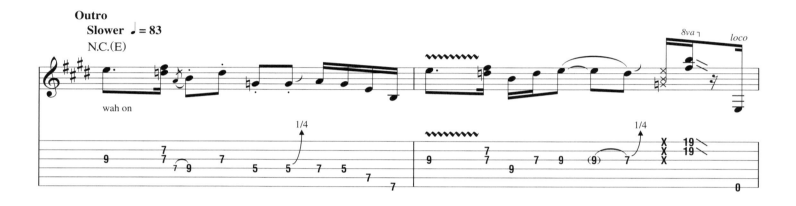

wah on

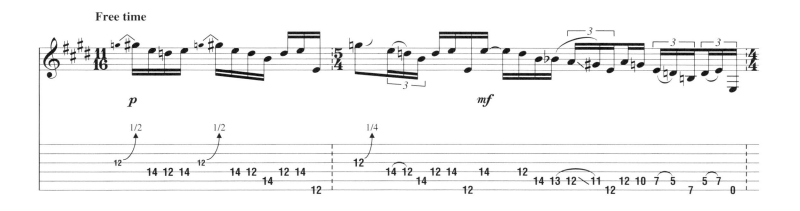

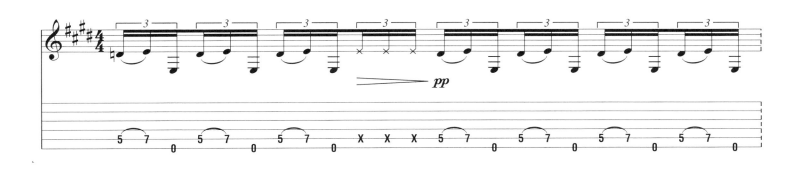

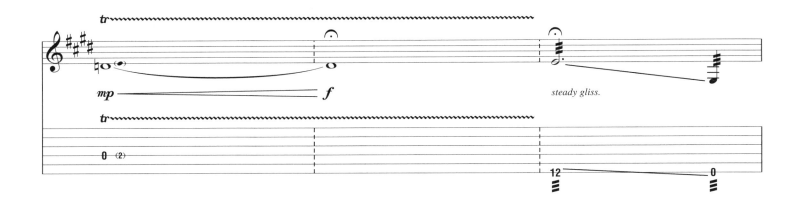

Free time

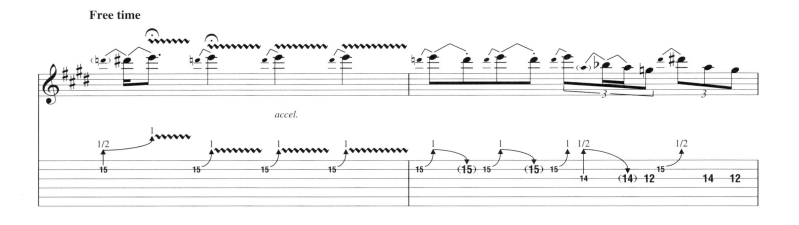

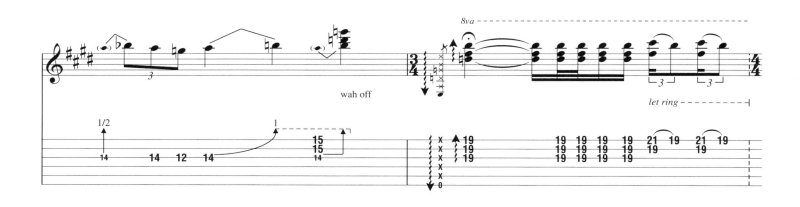

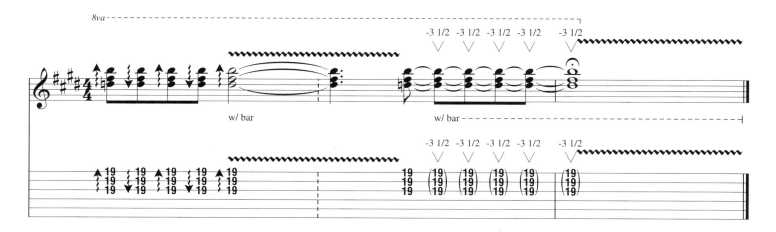

Wall of Denial

Written by Stevie Ray Vaughan and Doyle Bramhall

Tune down 1/2 step:
(low to high) E♭-A♭-D♭-G♭-B♭-E♭

Intro

Moderately ♩ = 116

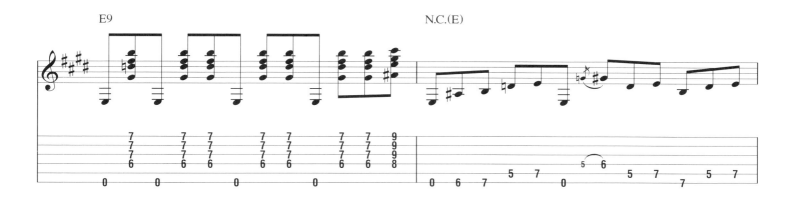

Verse

E9

1. A wall of ____ de - nial
2., 3. *See additional lyrics*

*3rd time, overdrive off

is fall - in' down. ____

To Coda ⊕

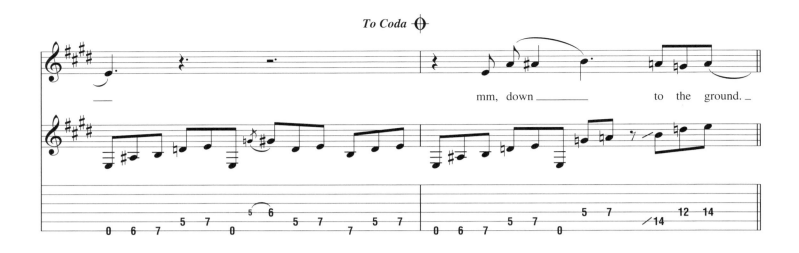

mm, down _____ to the ground. _

Guitar Solo

N.C.(E)

_f_

w/ overdrive pedal

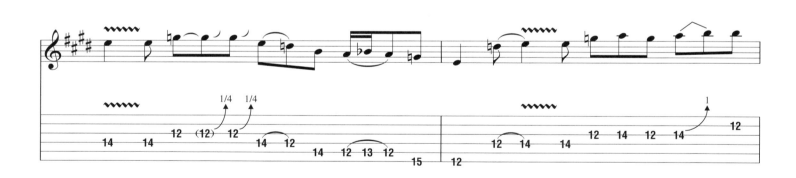

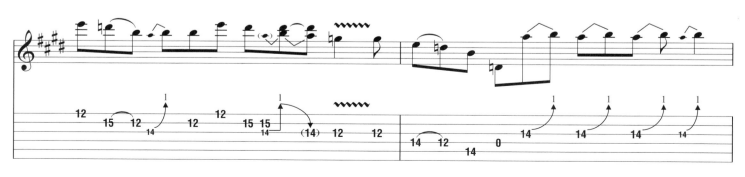

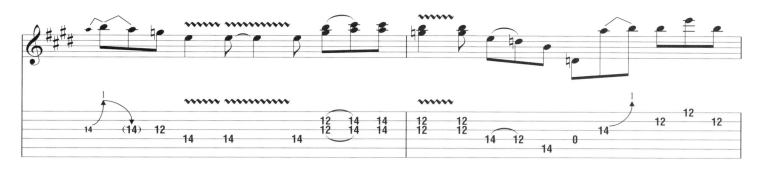

(A7)

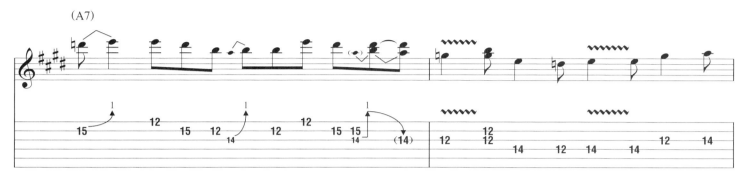

(G7)

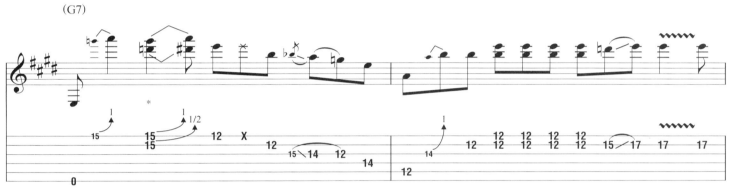

*Bend both notes with same finger.

(E)

* 2nd string sounds while caught under bending finger.

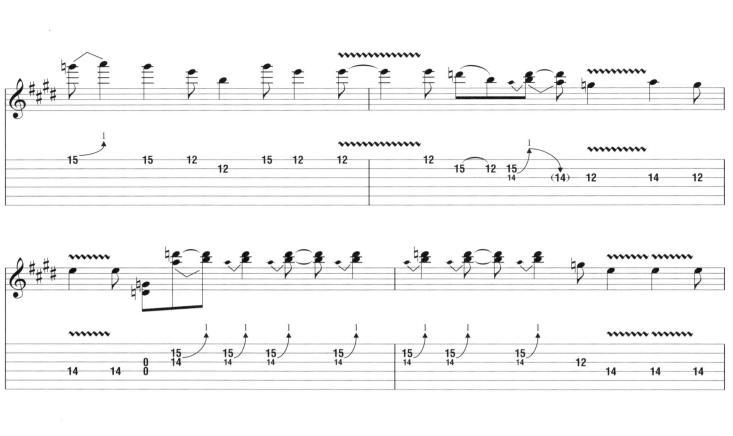

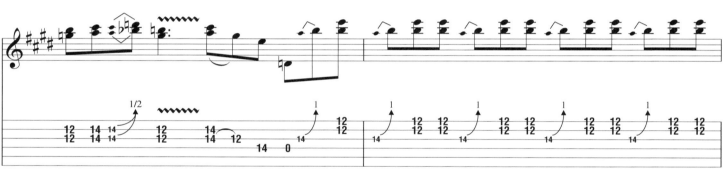

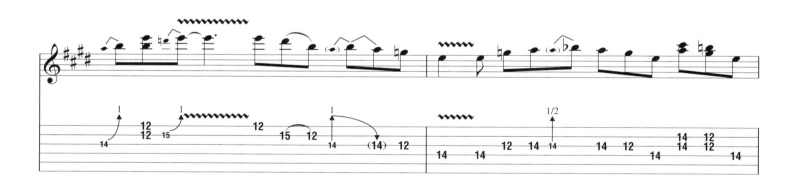

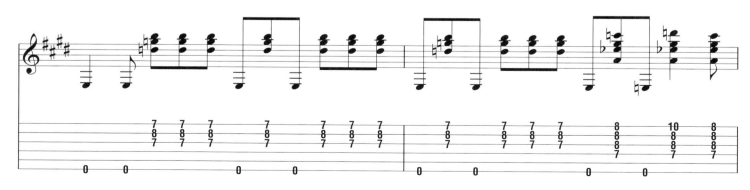

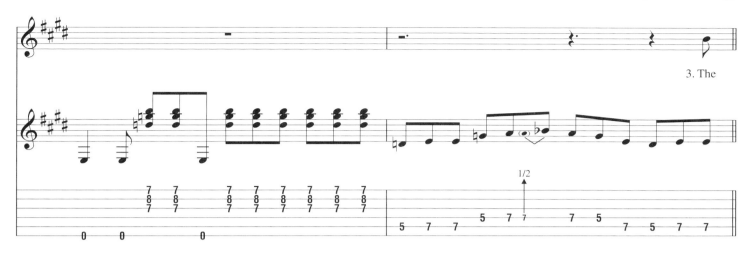

3. The

⊕ Coda

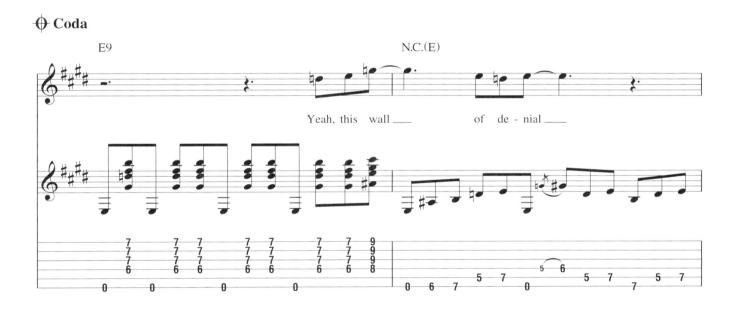

Yeah, this wall ___ of de - nial ___

must tum - ble down, down ___

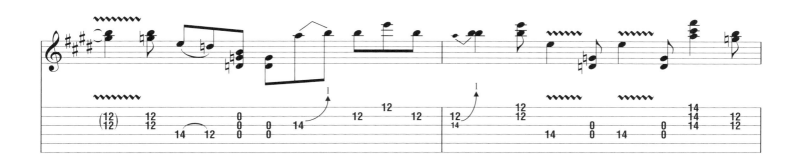

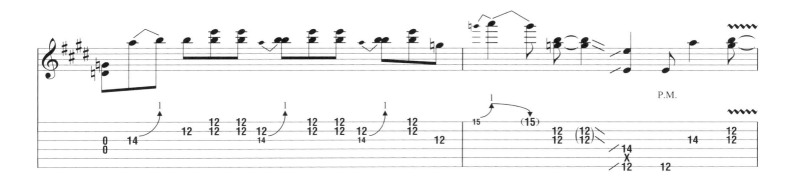

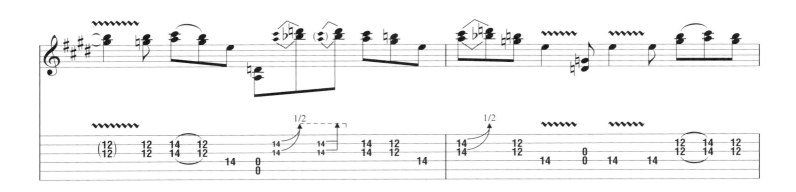

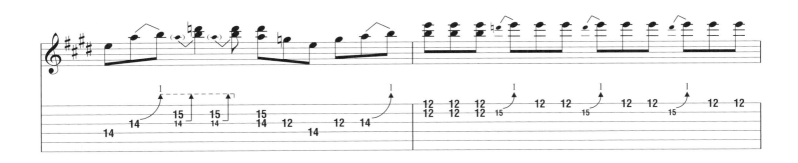

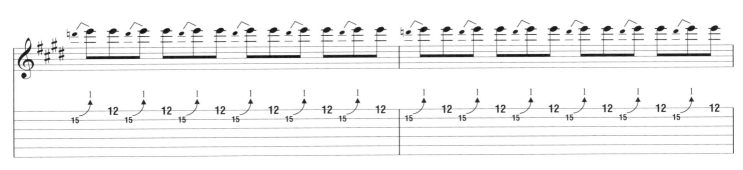

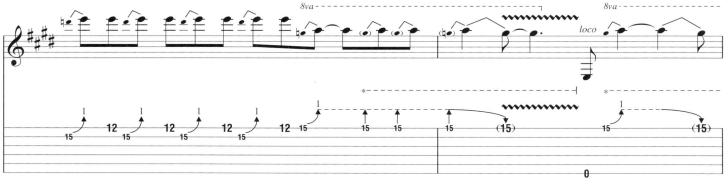

* 2nd string sounds while caught under bending finger, next 3 meas.

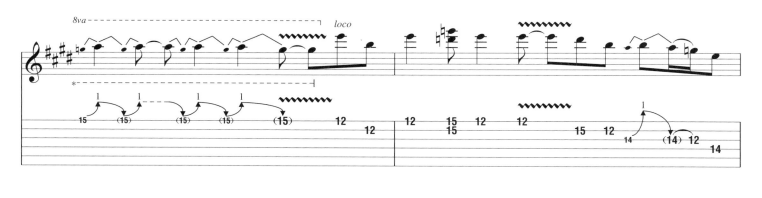

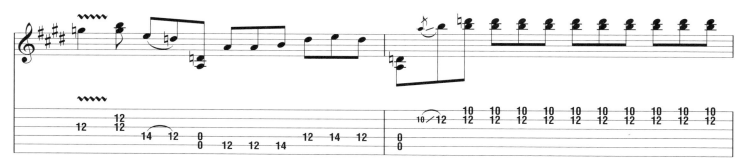

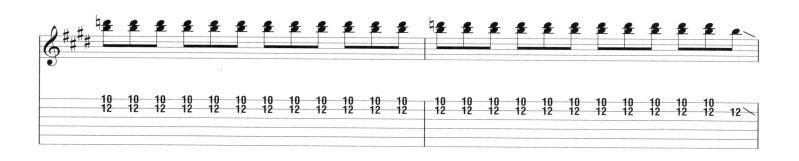

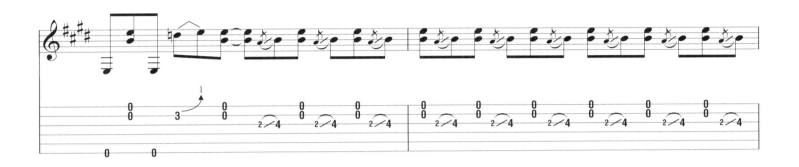

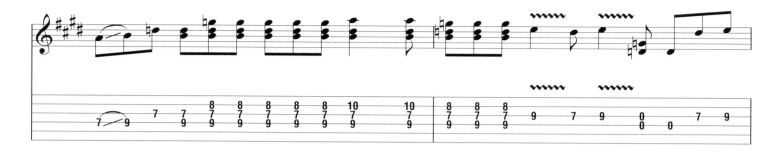

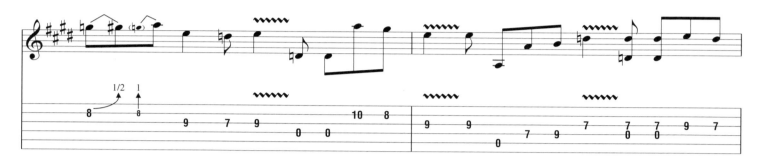

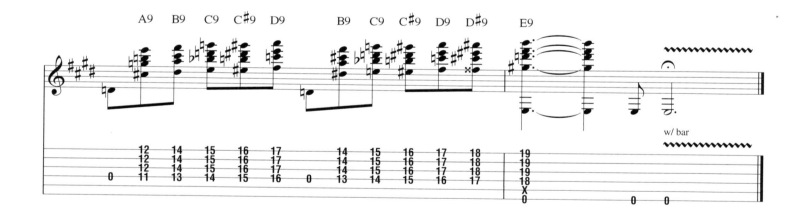

Additional Lyrics

2. We've all had our demons from the garden of white lies.
   Dressed them, amused them; pullin' wool over our eyes.
   Go so far as to love them, to keep from letting them go.
   All the while they were killin' us, but we couldn't let it show.

3. The simple things in life bring the greatest pleasure.
   A smile, a kiss, a little baby's laughter.
   It makes no difference if we run away in fear.
   The little things in life hold us so near.

This series will help you play your favorite songs quickly and easily. Just follow the tab and listen to the CD to hear how the guitar should sound, and then play along using the separate backing tracks. Mac or PC users can also slow down the tempo without changing pitch by using the CD in their computer. The melody and lyrics are included in the book so that you can sing or simply follow along.

1. ROCK
00699570 ....$16.99

2. ACOUSTIC
00699569.....................$16.95

3. HARD ROCK
00699573.....................$16.95

4. POP/ROCK
00699571.....................$16.99

5. MODERN ROCK
00699574 ....$16.99

6. '90s ROCK
00699572.....................$16.99

7. BLUES
00699575.....................$16.95

8. ROCK
00699585.....................$14.99

9. PUNK ROCK
00699576.....................$14.95

10. ACOUSTIC
00699586.....................$16.95

11. EARLY ROCK
0699579.....................$14.95

12. POP/ROCK
00699587.....................$14.95

13. FOLK ROCK
00699581.....................$15.99

14. BLUES ROCK
00699582.....................$16.95

15. R&B
00699583.....................$14.95

16. JAZZ
00699584.....................$15.95

17. COUNTRY
00699588.....................$15.95

18. ACOUSTIC ROCK
00699577.....................$15.95

19. SOUL
00699578.....................$14.99

20. ROCKABILLY
00699580.....................$14.95

21. YULETIDE
00699602.....................$14.95

22. CHRISTMAS
00699600.....................$15.95

23. SURF
00699635.....................$14.95

24. ERIC CLAPTON
00699649.....................$17.99

25. LENNON & McCARTNEY
00699642 ....$16.99

26. ELVIS PRESLEY
00699643.....................$14.95

27. DAVID LEE ROTH
00699645.....................$16.95

28. GREG KOCH
00699646.....................$14.95

29. BOB SEGER
00699647.....................$15.99

30. KISS
00699644.....................$16.99

31. CHRISTMAS HITS
00699652.....................$14.95

32. THE OFFSPRING
00699653.....................$14.95

33. ACOUSTIC CLASSICS
00699656.....................$16.95

34. CLASSIC ROCK
00699658.....................$16.95

35. HAIR METAL
00699660.....................$16.95

36. SOUTHERN ROCK
00699661.....................$16.95

37. ACOUSTIC METAL
00699662.....................$16.95

38. BLUES
00699663.....................$16.95

39. '80s METAL
00699664.....................$16.99

40. INCUBUS
00699668.....................$17.95

41. ERIC CLAPTON
00699669.....................$16.95

42. 2000s ROCK
00699670.....................$16.99

43. LYNYRD SKYNYRD
00699681.....................$17.95

44. JAZZ
00699689.....................$14.99

45. TV THEMES
00699718.....................$14.95

46. MAINSTREAM ROCK
00699722.....................$16.95

47. HENDRIX SMASH HITS
00699723.....................$19.95

48. AEROSMITH CLASSICS
00699724.....................$17.99

49. STEVIE RAY VAUGHAN
00699725.....................$17.99

50. 2000s METAL
00699726.....................$16.99

51. ALTERNATIVE '90s
00699727.....................$14.99

52. FUNK
00699728.....................$14.95

53. DISCO
00699729.....................$14.99

54. HEAVY METAL
00699730.....................$14.95

55. POP METAL
00699731.....................$14.95

56. FOO FIGHTERS
00699749.....................$15.99

57. SYSTEM OF A DOWN
00699751.....................$14.95

58. BLINK-182
00699772.....................$14.95

60. 3 DOORS DOWN
00699774.....................$14.95

61. SLIPKNOT
00699775.....................$16.99

62. CHRISTMAS CAROLS
00699798.....................$12.95

63. CREEDENCE CLEARWATER REVIVAL
00699802.....................$16.99

64. OZZY OSBOURNE
00699803.....................$16.99

65. THE DOORS
00699806.....................$16.99

66. THE ROLLING STONES
00699807.....................$16.95

67. BLACK SABBATH
00699808.....................$16.99

**68. PINK FLOYD –
DARK SIDE OF THE MOON**
00699809.....................$16.99

69. ACOUSTIC FAVORITES
00699810.....................$14.95

70. OZZY OSBOURNE
00699805.....................$16.99

71. CHRISTIAN ROCK
00699824.....................$14.95

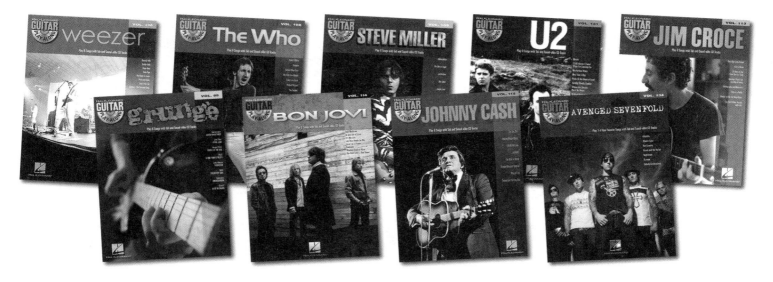

HAL•LEONARD® CORPORATION

7777 W. BLUEMOUND RD. P.O. BOX 13819 MILWAUKEE, WI 53213

For complete songlists, visit Hal Leonard online at
www.halleonard.com

Prices, contents, and availability subject to change without notice.

0712